OFF TRAIL

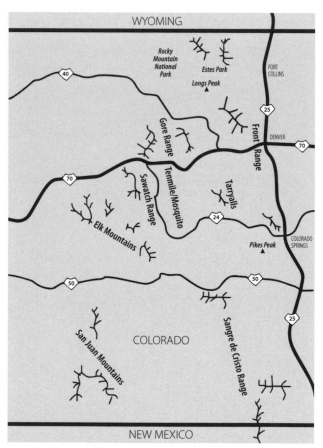

Map by Holli Schmitz. Copyright © 2017 by the University of Oklahoma Press.

OFF TRAIL

Finding My Way Home in the Colorado Rockies

Jane Parnell

UNIVERSITY OF OKLAHOMA PRESS : NORMAN

Portions of the following chapters appeared, in earlier forms and under the name Jane Koerner, in the publications noted here:

Chapter 1: "Adventuring on Colorado's Big Peaks," *High Country News,* August 19, 2011.

Chapter 2: "Gathering Strength on the Continental Divide," *High Country News,* September 14, 2012.

Chapters 4, 9, and 12: "Off Belay," *Mountain Gazette,* June 2011.

Chapters 14 and 17: "Pinned by a Boulder: A Contest with Quartzite—The Elk Range," in *Outdoors in the Southwest: An Adventure Anthology,* edited by Andrew Gulliford (Norman: University of Oklahoma Press, 2014).

Chapter 16: "The Lost Navigator," *High Country News,* October 27, 2015.

Chapter 17: "Why I Never Hike Alone," *High Country News,* June 29, 2012.

Chapter 18: "A Dog Named Beast," *Adventure Journal,* July 8, 2015, http://adventure-journal.com/2015/07/a-dog-named-beast/.

Library of Congress Cataloging-in-Publication Data

Name: Parnell, Jane, 1950– author.
Title: Off trail : finding my way home in the Colorado Rockies / Jane Parnell.
Description: Norman : University of Oklahoma Press, 2018.
Identifiers: LCCN 2017012736 | ISBN 978-0-8061-5900-3 (pbk. : alk. paper)
Subjects: LCSH: Parnell, Jane, 1950– | Women mountaineers—Colorado—Biography. | Hiking—Colorado.
Classification: LCC GV199.92.P383 A3 2017 | DDC 796.522092 [B]—dc23
LC record available at https://lccn.loc.gov/2017012736

The paper in this book meets the guidelines for permanence and durability of the Committee on Production Guidelines for Book Longevity of the Council on Library Resources, Inc. ∞

1 2 3 4 5 6 7 8 9 10

For RG, MEG, Alice Eugenia,
and Beast

I still vote civilization a nuisance, society a humbug,
and all conventionality a crime.

—Isabella Bird, 1874

Contents

Part II: After the Fall

Acknowledgments

In the tundra of the Colorado Rockies there are no trees and few man-made structures to help determine the scale of things and mark progress. The sun bears down, unfiltered. The inexperienced, solitary hiker can become disoriented and be forced to turn around. So it is with this book, my first. Without the insights and encouragement of many generous people, progress might have ground to a halt. And a project that began in graduate school might still be taking up space on my computer, unfinished, never to see the light of publication.

Among others, I thank Jennifer Sinor for pushing me where I most feared to go; Chris Cokinos for stressing the importance of giving natural history its proper due; Michael Sowder for instilling confidence in the power of unadorned nouns; Nadene LeCheminant for reining in my precious prose; Nancy Bentley for calling attention to what I left out; Diane "Musho" Hamilton and a host of other Zen masters for teaching me how to let go of my habitual handholds; and James M. Simson for helping me to recover from my fall.

Thanks also to historian Andrew Gulliford of Fort Lewis College for suggesting I query University of Oklahoma Press. Acquisitions editor Kathleen A. Kelly recognized the potential in the incomplete, rough draft I sent; Stephanie Evans shepherded the book through the editing and production process; Cleo Vastardis designed the book; and copyeditor Bonnie Lovell caught misspellings and other embarrassing errors.

I'm equally grateful for my hiking companions over the years, who deserve more recognition than was possible in this book. Without their support, some mountains on my list would have remained just that—unchecked names on a list. No companion was more constant and willing than my dog, Beast. For twelve summers he accompanied me on nearly every ascent. His enthusiasm remained undiminished by age and arthritis. The day this book began production proved his last, but not before he took one more walk around the yard.

PART I

The Chase

Alice: Would you tell me, please,
which way I ought to go from here?

The Cheshire Cat: That depends a
good deal on where you want to get to.

—Lewis Carroll, *Alice in Wonderland*

Solo

The file cabinet in my study houses my share of the topo maps. After the divorce, Karl and I split them fifty-fifty. For nearly fifteen years they ensured our safe passage, steering us around marshes and mine shafts, through cliff bands, to the top. Stained and torn now, they are missing vital pieces of information. When I remove them from their folders, they fall apart in my hands. I piece them back together with Scotch tape so I can spread them out on the carpet, and tantalize and torture myself with possibilities.

There are six hundred and thirty-eight mountains over thirteen thousand feet high in the Colorado Rockies. If I were sensible, it would take several lifetimes to do them all. But I want to climb them all in this lifetime, provided my joints will tolerate the punishment. I want to leave my mark—my signature in every summit register or glass jar left by a previous party. I want to possess these mountains as they possess me. I want to know everything about them—the density and condition of their forests; the scent and variety of their flowers; the angle, age, and condition of their rock; the size of their summits. I rank them by altitude and divide them into logical, achievable categories. One hundred and fifty highest. The bicentennials and tricentennials. The four hundred highest. I was the first woman to climb the one hundred highest peaks of Colorado; mathematical precision makes the remaining task more manageable.

From Memorial Day until the snow sticks, every weekend is dedicated to the peak-bagging objective, each triumphal date and my companions' initials recorded in the same notebook with a birdwatcher's fanaticism.

The solos with my most loyal companion, my dog, are signified with his nickname spelled backwards: God.

I hike for the exercise, burning off bad memories as if they were Christmas calories, transforming grief into muscle. "What's the rush? Are you training for an ultramarathon or something?" my friend asks when I return to camp an hour after he does. He turned back at timberline, exhausted by the pace I had set. It is my third summer without Karl, and I still have something to prove.

I hike for the thrill of it, scaring myself speechless on more than one occasion. But my body is up to it—legs of granite, heart and lungs a two hundred horsepower engine that drives me upward at eighteen hundred vertical feet per hour. Sixty-five heartbeats per second, three thousand six hundred per hour. On the trail my body ceases to be an object of curiosity or despair. It has a weight to it. My footsteps land lightly while my feet feel rooted. Every step a declaration of intimacy with the rock, the turf, the soil. The tapping of my hiking poles synchronizing with each inhalation and exhalation. My breath distilled into the clarity of light.

The divorce decree arrives in July, cementing our on-off separation of the past three years. Now it's official. Karl is no longer my guide, the expert with years more experience, a battering ram of a four-wheel drive, enough gear to equip a Himalayan expedition. The responsibility for transporting myself to the trailhead, for determining the routes and assessing the risks rests entirely on my shoulders.

Mummy Mountain, Rocky Mountain National Park, early August: I glance back at the dilating, bruised clouds and pick up the pace as I scramble up the last two hundred feet of the summit block, beating the lightning-charged cloudburst to the top by ten minutes. I outrun the storm's progression by choosing the correct shortcut down. Back at camp, I am welcomed by a Boy Scout troop leader who covets my spot for his party of ten. I'm happy to comply, confident I can beat nightfall, too, and make it out in time for a luxurious dining experience. No pine needles in the teacup. A steam-cleaned fork. USDA-certified beef on a porcelain plate. I don't want to break my dinner date with my parents, who rented a condo in Estes Park for the week. I told them I was hiking with a friend.

How do I explain that even though I am alone for the first time in my life, I am not as alone as they might assume? That I feel safer in the mountains on my own than among strangers in the city. That this is my belated rite of passage at age forty. I earned it; I paid for it—the scar tissue on my shins and in my heart a map of the interior topography of my life. Maps can be revised.

Pole Creek Mountain, San Juans, late August: Eight miles up Lost Creek, I find a safe place to cross, where the elk have flattened the bank and narrowed the channel with their habitual crossings. Their hoofprints in the mud provide stirrups for the leap to the other side. I land without a splash. Several hundred feet below the summit, another set of elk tracks guides me through the cliffs without a scratch. I will reach the top before the hailstorm and return to camp by lunchtime.

Uncompahgre Wilderness, mid-September: The *whoosh* of a low-flying hawk awakens me from a midafternoon nap in a basin beneath Mount Silver. It is three hours back to camp and the sun will set in two. The persistent bark of a coyote encourages me to keep moving. She is safeguarding her pups, spiriting me away from the den with the primeval song she spins out of thin air.

Cuatro Peak, Culebra Range, early October: A trail of fresh bear scat through the forest issues a warning. I'm trespassing on someone else's territory. I hustle along at warp speed even though I know it is not a grizzly. The last one in Colorado was killed by a poacher in 1979.

"You love the mountains more than you will love any man." A remark as hard to shake as a bruised toenail. Having announced my return to the condo in Estes with a *thunk* of shed boots, I am rewarded with Mother's best dish—fresh salmon marinated in soy sauce, lemon juice, and garlic—and some unsolicited advice. Her remark irritates me, and still does, because she is probably right. I don't know how to cope with the internet dating scene, where virtual specimens have replaced live ones. Rather than getting to know one another in increments over the course of our daily lives, waiting for the spark to combust spontaneously, we check each other out on Match.com and eHarmony. In a flurry of email exchanges, the candidates must be culled to a handful of must-meets who agree to a rendezvous site nowhere near my house in Colorado Springs.

The conversation with the architect who agreed to meet at Wild Oats comes to a halt when he looks down at my bandaged feet in the post-op sandals. He says he's running late for his doctor's appointment and he'll have to skip the coffee refill. We hadn't gotten to my mountaineering résumé yet, or the bunion surgery.

The accounting professor is willing to meet at my favorite Mexican restaurant in Denver, sixty-five miles away. He arrives first. I join him at the table next to the cash register. He orders chips with salsa. After the waitress delivers the order, he says, "I reserved a room for you at the motel across the street."

"Even the coyotes don't do it that quick."

"That's not what I meant. I thought you'd be too tired to drive home tonight. It's a long drive, isn't it? Especially at night." His Dos Equis is served. He squeezes the lime, squirting some of the juice onto his white shirt. He doesn't get the joke. Karl would have spit out his drink by now with his laughter.

"I'm not driving home tonight. I'm camping in the mountains." The chef put too many jalapeños in the salsa, and I'm on my second glass of ice water.

The enchiladas arrive, melted cheese still sizzling. He picks up his fork. "It's May. There will be snow up there. You're alone."

"My tent and sleeping bag are in my trunk." I look at his watch (mine cartwheeled into a creek) and excuse myself before the waitress brings dessert, saying, "Got to pitch that tent before dark." I do not tell him about my trophy collection, which is probably bigger than his and definitely covers more territory.

San Luis, Tijeras, Blanca Peaks. Pico Aislado, hidden away in a back valley, like the name suggests, with enough exposure to skip my customary self-portrait on the summit. Cyclone, Cirrus, and Oso, where a member of the Hayden survey of 1874 encountered a grizzly and lived to write about it. Heisspitz, Heisshorn, and Little Matterhorn, as if the Colorado Rockies were an extension of the Swiss Alps. Engineer, Galena, Eureka, Gold Dust, Crystal, Treasurevault, Lucky Strike, which isn't how I felt about it a century after the bust as I detoured around one collapsed mine shaft after another, dragging my mutt by the collar so he wouldn't be tempted by the arsenic-tainted water. Conundrum, Comanche, and that pragmatic compromiser, Ouray, who died before the forced relocation. Nathaniel Meeker, self-righteous Indian agent whose murder precipitated the banishment; and Kit Carson and Ulysses S. Grant scattered across three ranges on opposite ends of the state (one of those unintentional ironies of naming mountains for conquerors), while Arapaho and Navajo share a ragged ridge in the devastating wake of their defeat. The T's, the V's, the S's, the numbered and nameless peaks, my preference. A name conveys ownership. I wouldn't mind a Susan B. Anthony Peak. She toured Colorado in 1877 on behalf of the suffragist movement. Of all the mountains in my trophy collection, only a handful bear a woman's name. Silverheels, the nickname of an anonymous prostitute, seems prophetic in retrospect. She nursed the miners of Fairplay through a smallpox epidemic, forfeiting food and sleep, putting herself at risk as though their lives mattered more than hers. When she fell ill, rather than seek help, she covered her ruined face with a veil and vanished.

Obsessed and invisible: is that my lot in life, too?

I climb Silverheels twice: before the divorce and after with women friends who are also adjusting to changed circumstances. On the way down, when the terrain switches from talus to turf, we strip off our jackets and wrap them around our hips. Then we leap into the air and land on our sides and roll down the mountainside like potatoes spilled from a sack, tumbling to a stop in a bed of alpine forget-me-nots and moss campion cushions, unharmed. Marleen unbuttons her shirt. Annie clasps her hand to her mouth in a futile attempt to suppress a giggle. I rip off my clothes and they follow suit, a pack of alpha females intoxicated by their collective strength.

Weekdays I work to pay the bills, to convince myself I am capable of taking care of myself. Bruised legs and blistered lips retreat behind dark stockings and bright lipstick, deflecting criticism. My immaculate boss has high standards. The condition of my hair, sunburned and unruly, gets her attention. She suggests Redken's Extreme Conditioner. It fails to deliver on its promise—*restore your distressed hair to lustrous manageability*—and after noting the infraction in my biannual performance review, she hands me her hairdresser's business card. "Book an appointment."

During back-to-back integrated marketing meetings, while team leader Fred assigns the messages of the week—the same messages we've been trumpeting from sea to shining sea for three years—I confine my mental perambulations to pictographs in my notebook: Aztec pyramids with red dots to indicate the route of the sacrificial virgin; half circles for peaks with walkable trails; an anthropomorphic figure with an eagle head, human torso, and alpine sunflowers for hands. I keep my internal commentary to myself for fear of creating the wrong impression, stifling the howl in my throat, which could be misinterpreted as the wailing of self-imposed singlehood or the mating calls of Coyote Woman. Another strike against me in the performance review.

Weekend forays into the mountains compensate. The checkmarks in the margins of my peak-bagging list accumulate so fast, I can barely decipher one conquest from the next. As the triumphs mount, so do the accidental casualties. By the fourth anniversary of my divorce, my Honda Civic seems destined for the junkyard: two sets of tires replaced, not counting blown and shredded ones; a busted U-joint; the bumper drowned at a creek crossing in the San Juan Mountains. The one hundred thousand mileage marker on the odometer resets to zero, restarting the journey.

On my return home, the face confronting me in the bathroom mirror after the shower resembles Alice on her return from Wonderland, bright-eyed with astonishment and fatigue, revisiting her question after tumbling down the rabbit hole and nearly drowning in her own pool of tears: "If I'm not the same . . . who in the world am I?"

And yet not one mishap. Fifteen to twenty summits a summer, and I lose my way only once without having to sacrifice the summit, my sense of direction corrected by a thorough review of the topo map. After several summers of hiking with friends or alone, I can recognize the tingle of electricity on my scalp in time to dodge an incoming lightning bolt, identify a peace-loving skunk in the dark, and find a summit in the fog; but I lose my Honda Civic in the grocery store parking lot. The orienteering course offered by the Colorado Mountain Club does nothing to minimize my disorientation in town. I am dyslexic with street signs, especially where I used to live, in Manitou Springs at the foot of Pikes Peak. Mountain Meadow? Deer Path? Elk Park? The names conflict with the Kentucky bluegrass lawns and domestic cats sunning themselves in raised petunia beds.

After a lengthy absence, I finally test my orienteering skills in Manitou Springs. I park my car with the Texans and Oklahomans in the public lot behind Patsy's popcorn stand and the Penny Arcade, and walk the crooked, hilly streets for hours on end, until my stamina gives out. I start out at dusk, when most of the tourists have already packed it in for the night. The camera dangling from my neck labels me as one of them. As I stroll up Manitou Boulevard, I barely recognize the intersection with the street where I used to live. My customary landmark half a block up, Filthy Wilma's painted face on the brick exterior of my favorite vintage clothing shop, is gone. The sign over the doorway says, "Greenhouse Gallery: A Co-Op of Manitou Artists." I've never heard of any of them.

I head up the avenue, ducking my head as I pass the window display of muskets aimed at the Mexican restaurant across the street, and beyond that block proceed, my head held high, through a law-abiding neighborhood of renovated bungalows and former boardinghouses converted into stately homes, not pausing once until I reach the gate at the bottom of the staircase. The gate won't budge. Its uppermost hinge has separated from the post, and the gate is too loose to swing through the pile of mildewed leaves on the other side. I lift the gate by its ornamental crest and push; it gives a few inches with a screech of iron on battered concrete, shoving the leaves out of the way. Beyond the gate is a steep staircase buried in more leaves. Seventy-two steps in all. A number I memorized shortly after Karl and I moved into the house.

Seventy-two steps. Steep and narrow with three forty-five-degree turns. I take a deep breath and begin the ascent. The slap, slap, slap of running sneakers on asphalt stops me in my tracks and spins me around. There she is—my successor, the Nordic goddess, perpetual youth. Coppertoned skin glistening with sweat, bared abs taut and rippling, twin greyhounds trotting along on her right and left, eyeing the street riffraff ahead. I know it is her because Karl has boasted of the dogs' racing pedigree. She races by in skintight, sky-blue Nike polyester, the greyhounds in lockstep. She must be training for the Pikes Peak marathon. Karl runs it every August.

I retrace my route, pausing to admire the cotton and silk imports in the window of Casual Comforts before turning onto the boulevard. Half a block farther, on the other side of the street, Patsy's is still open for business even though no customers are lined up at the order window. I cross the footbridge behind Patsy's and stroll down the alley, into the Penny Arcade. It takes me nearly twenty minutes to find Zambini, the Fortune Teller. Between the throngs of tattooed, spike-haired teens and the rat-a-tat-tat of their intergalactic dogfights, I am hopelessly confused. But after asking the night manager for directions three times, I finally find Zambini in a dusty, dim corner of the antique room. I drop a quarter into the slot and wait for Zambini's turbaned head to fix me in its red-eyed stare.

I must have been his first customer in years. His voice warbles as if swimming from the bottom of a fish tank or awakening from a century-long nap.

"Look into my crystal ball," he commands.

He holds the ball in his hands. With a clank, a card pops out of the metallic slit in his shirt pocket. He orders me to take it.

"Your lucky color is green." He got that one half right. I have hazel eyes. In the sunlight, green flecks speckle the brown irises. Several blind dates have been complimentary. They say my eyes are my best feature.

I fritter away a wallet full of quarters until the fortune I am seeking finally slides out of Zambini's pocket. "Unlucky in love? Your luck will change but only if you stop looking in the usual places."

I consult my topo maps. They rarely let me down as long as I hold them to the light so I can distinguish fingerprints and watermarks from contour lines and genuine summits. Their names and histories compose a haunting tune that plays, night after night, in vaguely remembered dreams. Cyclone, Precarious, Broken Hand, Crystal, Purgatoire, and Lookout. Bartlett, still standing after numerous beheadings to feed the global construction market. Vestal and Ice Mountain, lumped together in my mind's eye despite their separation of several hundred miles to remind myself of the psychological risks of excessive solitude. Unhappily celibate and hardened in old age.

The summers pass in a whirl of serial conquests indistinguishable from one season to the next.

I'll hike until the joints in my big toes dislocate and the podiatrist orders me to take three months off to recover from bunion surgery. The screws in my feet compromise their flexibility, and I learn how to scramble on stiff arches and rigid toes.

I'll hike until the vision in my left eye clouds over, and I stumble into my ophthalmologist's office, complaining of the blinding light in my eyes when I drive. He schedules cataract surgery.

"What about the cobwebs in my eyes?" I ask during my first exam since the surgery.

"Floaters. An exceptional number for someone your age," he says. "It has nothing to do with the surgery. Between your myopia and ultraviolet-light exposure, you've got the eyesight of an eighty-year-old." He spares both of us the lecture. I passed him once on the trail; he was equipped with only a fanny pack. I was headed down; he had just left the parking lot. He was moving so fast in his jogging attire, I thought he was pursuing a long-lost lover.

I'll hike until my heart stops beating and they find me belly up in the talus, my rictus grin a warning to those who venture out on their own.

Until then I'll hike sideways and with baby steps and thousand-dollar knee braces if I must. "We can keep you going a while longer with physical therapy and ice packs and rooster comb injections," the orthopedist says after showing me the MRIs. "Climbing is brutal on your joints. Eventually, you'll have to have both knees replaced. Have you considered taking up cycling and swimming?"

"Will I be able to climb with artificial joints?"

"They'll last a lot longer if you avoid high-impact activity."

I'll take his advice about reducing the elevation gains and mileage. But my feet won't cooperate. They cover so many miles while I sleep, my twitching toes wake me up before the alarm goes off, ready to hit the trail again. I tumble out of bed, onto the floor. It's Monday morning. I have to go to work.

2

Continental Divide

"Three hundred more miles," Alice shouts, beating me, her eight-year-old kid sister, to the punch. We've been clocking the mileage since Salina, Kansas, pleading for updates every ten minutes. The closer we get to the Colorado border, the more agitated the sea of wheat becomes in the face of a stiff wind. We steady the swaying of our station wagon with our songs. Before the border crossing, we sing, *Home, home on the range, where the deer and the antelope play,* forgetful of their absence; and then, after a respectful break for the sake of our father at the wheel, *Oh my darling, Oh my darling, Oh my darling, Clementine, you are lost and gone forever, dreadful sorry, Clementine,* our hearts brimming rather than broken, the windmills spinning as we fly past, the grain elevators nosing the sky. Beyond Oakley, Kansas, Mother spots the real mountains—a streak of cumulus on the horizon. Snow in August! It is August 1959, and the sky hangs over us violet blue, undiluted by the smudge of burning coal that will fuel the expansion of Front Range cities once the rest of the heartland grows restive.

Snow in August! The Continental Divide of my childhood rises up the moment I spy the fractured, uplifted horizon formed by the Rocky Mountains. Ahead lie Longs Peak and the alpine meadow where my sister and I will play hide-and-seek in the willows below our rented cabin. Ahead lie weeks full of freedom and possibility.

Left behind, so close to Missouri it barely qualifies as Kansas: our neighborhood in Prairie Village, neither a prairie nor a village, but a postwar housing development on the outskirts of Kansas City. A chain-link fence keeps runaways like me out of the concrete creek bed behind our house. It looks like every other house in the neighborhood except for the red shingles and shutters, and the absence of a basketball hoop over the garage door. Troops of boys patrol our street, dispensing vigilante justice to outlaws, undaunted by the chiggers in their socks and the damp heat that could render them delirious or conjure a tornado out of a becalmed sky. Gangs of girls gather in upstairs bedrooms, cooling themselves off with paper fans as they mother their Barbie dolls to perfection. They cover their featureless, inanimate bodies in gold brocade or pink satin, any hint of nonconformity or curiosity smothered by their big blonde hair.

My dolls reside in cardboard shoeboxes, three decapitated corpses to a casket.

Frosty McGee is equally at home with both tribes. During the school year I study him at the lunch table to see how he pulls it off. His blue eyes gaze into mine without blinking. He has freckles and a softness of manner that invites girl talk, and I am not the only girl in Miss Lund's third-grade class with a crush. All the other girls at the table flirt shamelessly with him. I keep my infatuation to myself. If I betray my true feelings, Martha Gunther will humiliate me in public. "Jane's in love with Frosty! Jane's in love with Frosty!"

The bell rings. The savages mop up the slaughtered remains of their meal with their last slice of Wonder bread before they're rounded up and herded back to class. Miss Lund stares us into silence. Our eyes follow her to the blackboard. She turns her back and chalks a sentence for us to diagram. Frosty McGee passes a note to Patty Lindquist. With a blush she scribbles a response, reaches across the aisle, and tucks his amended note into the back pocket of his pants. Frosty has fallen for Patty.

It's hopeless. I will never measure up.

I am Bucky Four-Eyes, cursed for all time by buck teeth and thick eyeglasses finned in rhinestone-specked black. I am an unclassifiable freak. With my sunken sternum—pigeon's breast Dr. Jeffries calls it—I can't defend myself from Martha's X-ray vision. "Who stomped on you? Daffy Duck?" she says at recess, seeing right through my sister's hand-me-down blouse. "You'll never grow a decent pair of boobs." For the rest of the school year, I take myself out of the picture with hunched shoulders, comically outsized clothing, and an outbreak of eczema in my scalp.

School over, my prospects improve with the formation of a Texas Ranger unit in my cousins' neck of the neighborhood. It isn't the odor of my sulfur shampoo that disqualifies me but the butchered bangs that brand my forehead like an alien longhorn. I should have asked Mother to trim my bangs—she had a steadier hand—but she would have disapproved of the style I had in mind. A crewcut. What her sewing scissors couldn't alter, the bobby pins in her jewelry box might subdue.

The Texas Rangers size me up, label me "it," and hunt me down in the forsythias. I beg for mercy half-heartedly. It is thrilling to be the center of attention, until they drag me across the crabgrass and stake me to the ground by the wrists and ankles. My captors are as ruthless as the Apache in John Ford westerns. Even the sky shows no mercy with its quivering heat, blooming clouds, and flying insects.

The shoe laces binding my wrists have compromised the blood supply to my fingers. My hands writhe in protest, arousing the curiosity of the crows on the power line. They stop squabbling and watch to the bitter end. My tethered legs, which are splayed like a dissected frog in my sister's biology class. The ants crawling under my shirt, marching into my underpants as beads of sweat collect in the fist-sized depression in my defective chest.

What was my offense?

"You're a girl," says Cousin Phil, the youngest of my three tormentors. Before leaving me to the ants, he kneels beside my head to tighten the shoelaces around my wrists.

The crows on the power line have turned their backs to watch the blue jay in the oak tree. I look up at the broken sky. The heat has blown apart the cumulus clouds. The clouds drip with perspiration. I pray for the sirens to go off, for a funnel to swirl out of the melting sky. It will scatter the boys like cottonwood seeds and scoop me up with its flicking, pallid green tail, holding me tight until it sets me down at the foot of the Rocky Mountains.

I do not belong to either tribe.

The screen door flies open. "Henry Lee! Philip Travis!" The Texas Rangers are nowhere in sight, having long since departed on another mission to enforce the pecking order. The door bangs shut. Footsteps crunch across the scorched grass. Aunt Lucille will free me.

My mother picks me up and, out of respect for my feelings perhaps, asks no questions on the drive home. The moment the car rolls to a stop in our driveway, I leap out and make a beeline for the basement, where my father often falls asleep on the sofa. He would sleep all day if it weren't for the western matinees on television and the bottle of Cutty Sark on the coffee table. On the label a ship with giant sails is tossed about by cresting waves. The ship is as restless as he is.

The sofa is vacant. The dent in the pillow suggests my father slept here recently. I run upstairs and push open the door to their bedroom. My father is asleep in his own bed. I try not to startle him as I lie down beside him and rest my head on the pillow of his stomach. I try to stay awake so when he wakes up, I will hear him when he tells me he loves me, not once but three times—our ritual. If he says it enough times, I will believe him.

Weeknights my sister and I are in bed when he comes home from work. But on Friday nights he tries to make it home in time for another ritual. Whistling a danceable tune, he picks me up by the shoulders and twirls me around the kitchen. I grip the tops of his patent-leather shoes with my bare toes to compensate for the inadequacy of my arms, which are too short to reach around his waist. Our waltz proceeds at a stiff-legged gait; despite our mismatched embrace we stick together to the last whistled note. I would dance with him until my toes bleed, but he cuts the routine short, exhausted by another ten-hour workday.

After church on Sundays, he takes us on drives through the countryside. No street signs for guidance, acres and acres of plowed prairie swirling with tractor-spewed dust, an occasional farmhouse with a bleached barn, a sky that dwarfs the landscape. Dad always finds his way back, his sixth sense infallible.

In Rocky Mountain National Park, the mountains hug me tight, sheltering me from harm. They pinch the sky into a faint ribbon of blue, shutter the meadow below our rented cabin at Bowen Woods in intermittent shadow and silence. I learn to predict the weather by watching for subtle changes in cloud cover and light. One mountain distinguishes itself from the rest of the range with its singular height, flat top, and precipitous east face: Longs Peak. A black halo above the peak foreshadows a sudden temperature drop and an afternoon shower. After the shower, badgers poke their heads out, noses on high alert. Butterflies, lighter than lace, flick the air lilac. I want to fly with them, Huck Finn plotting his escape.

From the front step of our cabin at Bowen Woods, I study Longs Peak in the crystalline brightness of morning, as elk graze in the meadow below. At this time of day, the mountain seems closer and less formidable than it is. But in the graying dimness of a gathering storm, it retreats, a puzzle with missing pieces. If I am patient, the clouds will lift, revealing a dusting of snow. Sometimes the mountain emerges from the mist—its dome gold or polished silver. The aftermath of each storm short-lived and surprising, at sunset the color of the mountain determined by the density of the cloud cover.

A trail runs through the meadow. I interpret the thud of horse hooves as another search party in progress. The rangers must be approaching to fetch Fred Bowen, the caretaker, from his woodpile. He is a consummate mountaineer who has probably climbed more peaks in the park than any of the rangers. But instead of rangers, a train of tourists passes by, Brownie cameras pocketed, so the straps don't catch on their saddle horns and dismount them. The wrangler sits on the lead quarter horse cockeyed, as if dozing in his saddle.

Fred Bowen is as diligent with the woodcutting as Mother with the cooking on the finicky, wood-burning stove. Scabs and bruises decorate his hands, the bronze medals of his profession. When he isn't pounding a loose nail back into place or scrubbing the chimneys to our stoves, he is chopping wood and stacking it in tidy piles. By the end of our stay, more than enough wood will be stacked outside the main cabin to see him and his wife, Ruth, through the winter. He is a man of few words and ceaseless activity who has little time for children and their questions. Yet I would rather watch him at work than hang out with playmates my age or coax Alice outside. He is beholden to no one; he gets the job done. He built all the cabins at his plainspoken, modest resort in Hollowell Park, hauling the downed timber from the hillside out back. The park service contacts him after a disappearance or an accident, and he hauls those bodies out, too, if necessary. One of his retrievals slipped while soloing the East Face of Longs Peak. As he lay on a ledge, drifting in and out of consciousness, a witness shouted down at him, "Hang on. Help is on the way." By the time Fred arrived on the scene, the climber had rolled off the ledge.

"Never hike alone," Fred told us on his return. And that was all he had to say about the accident. If he grieved the untimely demise of this unfortunate young man, he expressed it with the swing of an axe against wood.

Mother is reluctant to let us play in the meadow again. We might drown in the creek or wander into the woods—bear habitat, no place for children. "Nonsense," Fred says. "Dress them in red jackets so you can keep track of them. And insist they stay out in the open."

The forest and willow ban make hide-and-seek impractical. We brainstorm an alternative. We will create a kingdom befitting Lewis Carroll's Red King and Queen. Gopher mounds mark the four corners of the realm. We raid the scarlet gilia for silken trumpets for the royal procession. We pluck a thistle and adorn our Red Queen with an enormous coneflower hat. She wilts.

Alice picks up a stick and rubs it in a thicket of pungent sagebrush. "A potent fragrance for reviving the queen. We should court her favor because she is easily miffed and rather unforgiving." Then she waves her wand over my head. "And for you to cast a spell over the walrus in the woods. Children are his oysters. He spits their bones out after eating them. See those pebbles in the creek?"

I turn to look.

"Tag, you're it," she shouts, dashing for the nearest cover, the willows farther up the creek.

"We're not playing that game, Alice. Remember our promise to Mother?"

Beyond Mother's watchful eye, Alice seems emboldened. Without a backward glance, she keeps moving, unhearing or defiant. I don't recognize this Alice. The Alice I know is eager to please, loathe to express a contrary opinion, Aunt Alice's agreeable personality. How easily she ingratiated herself with the girls. Her tribal membership undisputed because of her devotion to her dolls, her love of feminine colors, and her pitch-perfect singing.

"Alice, where are you?"

The opening Alice slipped through has closed. My eyes search for her red jacket in a mass of branches that whipsaw and sigh and gnarl. The Red King could be standing in the entryway and I wouldn't see it.

All is forgiven when my parents realize I'm the one who reined her in and brought her home. Her kid sister. Hilarious. They can hardly wait to tell our grandparents.

Would they have named her after Mother's only sister had they foreseen? Alice who went through the looking glass and got lost in the woods and met up with Tweedledum and Tweedledee, while the Red King was napping under a tree.

It's getting dark, and she doesn't know which way to go. Can they tell her? They make her cry with their preposterous non-answers.

When the Red King wakes up, says Dee, "Where will you be? . . . Nowhere! Why you're only some sort of thing in his dream."

"You know very well you're not real," says Dum.

3

Queen of the Mountain

The spider is suspended in space, his rope a golden thread in the lenses of the binoculars. His partner crouches on a ledge below, feeding him the rope that is supposed to save his life if he falls—provided the pitons and belay bolt stay put.

They waver in and out of view. The weight of the binoculars is winning the wrestling match with my tentative nine-year-old's grip. My father urges me to persevere; I will be rewarded for my effort. I will witness history—or disaster. The wrangler in charge of our horse party intervenes, steering the lenses, adjusting their focus.

Cars line both sides of the highway below. Binoculars, opera glasses, rented telescopes are all trained on the same spot: the unconquered Diamond dominating the East Face of Longs Peak. The Holy Grail of technical alpine climbing in the Rockies, the Diamond in August 1960 remains the last holdout as less-challenging routes succumb in the wake of post–world war technological advancements. Stettner's Ledges, the Window, the Diagonal—none of these routes on the East Face approximate the sheerness and length of the Diamond, nearly one thousand feet of vertical and overhanging granite. Climbers nationwide covet the prize. Skeptics say it will never be climbed.

Bombarded with applications, the park service finally grants permission to a schoolteacher and a PhD student from California. Their climbing résumé was persuasive: first ascents on Yosemite's El Capitan, ambitious routes in the Tetons. The duo has been training for months, waiting for the park service to give the go-ahead. They've stockpiled gear, recruited a support party, studied the most promising lines.

Cries of indeterminate origin travel across the forested flank of Longs Peak, dying out in midair. "They're yodeling!" the wrangler exclaims, hoisting his cowboy hat in approval.

"Yogeling?"

"Singing like us cowboys only with an accent," he says as he readjusts the position of the binoculars in my hands. Spiderman has moved an inch up the crack. The legs of his seated companion dangle off the ledge.

"They're happy?" I ask.

"Maybe yodeling gives them the courage to keep going," my father says.

Spectators who camped overnight or rode up at dawn place bets on the outcome, the fatalists outnumbering the optimists. His rope blending in, Spiderman inches toward a deeper crack, propelled by invisible limbs. Then he vanishes. The mountain has swallowed him. Horns honk. The spectator with the worst sunburn says, "That's the last we'll see of him."

"I hope he has life insurance," his wife says. "He's married."

Dad opens the sack lunch Mother prepared before sending us on our way and inhales two peanut butter sandwiches. A chipmunk gobbles up stray crumbs as he takes a swig from his Orange Crush.

We slathered ourselves in sun cream for the ride up. Now my sister is shivering in the shower of windblown leaves that frequently precedes a storm. The storm is already forming on the peak. Patches of mist swirl around the summit, swelling and congealing as they drift downward. Our wrangler retrieves a sweater from his saddle pack. The rest of the tourists in our party are determined to stay until Spiderman crawls out of his lair.

Before our departure this morning, Fred Bowen predicted another night on the mountain for the team. I picture them huddled together, down jackets for blankets, a ledge for a mattress, the Milky Way their only lamp.

"Who will rescue them if they don't make it to the summit?" I ask. Fred Bowen could have answered my question, but he stayed behind to attend to his chores.

The threat of a storm turned them back yesterday, forcing them down to the ledge where they had stored their bivy gear. Hunkering down for the night, they waited for the sun to light the route they established with a fixed line for their second attempt. Even in good weather, the climb could not be completed in one day, as they had hoped. The fragility of the rock took them by surprise. From below, it looked solid, receptive to the hammering in of their pitons. But the higher they climbed, the flakier the rock.

"They can't retreat again," reports a Yosemite veteran who camped here overnight so he could observe the entire ascent. "The ranger says they've run out of rope."

Through the binoculars being passed back and forth, we confirm our worst fears: the angle of the ever-steepening face exceeds vertical, and Spiderman is climbing in a partial backbend like a weary gymnast. I wonder how they switch leads without entangling themselves. I wonder how they convince themselves to keep going when the rock grows wet and it isn't raining and they have to climb through a waterfall of melting ice. I wonder what they say to each other when the clouds pile up, threatening yet another storm. *Did we make the wrong decision?* I wonder if they go numb with fear and the cold when they encounter several blocks of ice, hundreds of feet above Chasm Lake, where more spectators are gathered, watching through binoculars, calculating the odds, cracking jokes.

In newspaper photos of their arrival on the summit the next day, they look exhausted and emaciated, not triumphant. The reporters applaud as Spiderman's wife greets him with a kiss and a chocolate bar.

The victory parade is an impromptu affair. Perhaps the rangers bet against them, anticipating a hopeless, military-style rescue operation. Despite the short notice, hundreds of natives and tourists alike turn out for the celebration. I picture the victors in the lead car of the rodeo parade, waving through a blizzard of confetti, the whine of their convertible drowned out by cascading cheers.

The hill behind our cabin must have a summit somewhere beyond the boulders and ponderosas. I slip out the back door, while my sister remains on the sofa, inclined as always to stay within calling distance of Mother, who forgot to latch the screen door. I shut it softly so she won't hear me, not that she could hear me over the whistling of the kettle on the wood-burning stove.

I ran away once before—in Prairie Village. Packed up my suitcase with my stuffed animal collection and four pairs of clean socks, and bolted out the front door in plain sight of Mother, who looked up from her Agatha Christie to inquire, "Do you have enough socks?" When I reached the boulevard at the bottom of our street, I turned back, reined in by Mother's frequent admonition: Never cross a busy street without an adult.

At Bowen Woods she took extra precautions in case of a reoccurrence, zipping me up in my red nylon jacket before letting me out to play. This time I zipped myself up, pocketing the biscuit I didn't eat for breakfast. There was no salami in the cooler, no chocolate anywhere in the cabin.

I didn't anticipate the gravel. Instinctively I lean outward to counteract the ankle-turning slippage and start side-hilling like the elk do when they ascend from the meadow into the forest. Hummingbirds buzz by in flashes of iridescent green. The trunks of the ponderosas soar beyond my range of vision, their uppermost branches lost in the sky like Jack's beanstalk. The lichen-splattered boulders look like they could come to life at any moment and speak—trolls from the underworld conspiring with Mother to warn me away from the forest. But I am not afraid because the spidermen who conquered the Diamond were not afraid. I will climb a boulder, and when I reach the top, I will shout triumphantly at the top of my lungs, letting the whole world know of my achievement. I reach for a handhold, then another, my feet secure on the bottom ledge. Halfway up, I slip on the spongy lichen. This must be how hummingbirds learn to fly. They have to test their wings, not once but many times. I pick myself up, dusting off the gravel and retrieving my glasses, so I can see well enough to hike beyond the boulder. On the other side, a narrow shelf in the rock leads to the top. I rely on my legs until the last move, too much of a stretch without using my arms.

I am not afraid of the height. The chipmunks have crowned me queen of the boulder, their forepaws extended for the royal dispensation. I share the crumbling crust of my biscuit, but it fails to satisfy their hunger, and they scamper into my lap and stand on their haunches, scratching at my jacket. I could shake them off, but they are my devoted subjects, their teeth as prominent as mine.

The search party finds me beneath the umbrella of a ponderosa, napping on a bed of pine needles. They spotted my red jacket. I do not want to be rescued. Mother's injunction forgotten, I have conquered her fear of the forest and its predators. Now I can vanquish the dark and sleep here overnight.

"Snack time," Dad says, bending over to brush the pine needles from my hair. "Mom baked peanut butter cookies."

I can smell the peanut butter on her fingers as she holds the screen door open, the white bomb of the hot water heater behind her gurgling in preparation for my hot shower.

For the rest of our vacation my scrambles must be confined to the roof of our cabin. From there I can look down on Alice and boss her around until caught and ordered down. "Come on up, Alice. It's easy. The logs overlap on the corner. Plenty of room for your hands and feet." Her attention has drifted somewhere else. She is frozen in place, her eyes turned inward, fixed on some imaginary place I cannot penetrate.

Dad, a Western history buff, gives me a nickname that sustains me not only throughout the school year but adolescence, especially during lunchtime debates with Martha Gunther and the rest of the cheerleaders. Which shade of lipstick—Peach Blush or Cherry Kiss—will bag a suitor bearing a silver ID bracelet? Who cares? I am Jane Clark, precocious explorer—until Martha extends her arm so that everyone at the table can examine her bracelet. It is engraved with Dusty's name, the sandy-haired captain of the basketball team. A gasp of admiration—or is it envy?—engulfs our table. Martha stares at my wrist and eliminates the competition with one remark. "You don't have a sweetheart. Your bracelet is blank. You bought it yourself at the dime store. I was with you."

In the daydreams of my teens and twenties, I often return to Bowen Woods, even though by then the conservation-minded park service had evicted private property owners like Fred and Ruth Bowen, and the cabins were occupied by seasonal rangers. In subsequent summers we stayed at the Y camp, sacrificing our view of Longs Peak. Eventually the cabins at Bowen Woods were demolished; not one nail can be found today.

In my daydreams one cabin has survived the bulldozing: ours. The front window is empty, its splintered glass ground into the gravel, but the front door is still attached to the hinges. It opens easily. The door handle and lock are gone. The floorboards inside are too rotten for entry. I sit in the doorway, dangling my feet where the front step used to be as I warm myself in the sun. The grass in the meadow is the color and texture of mountain lion fur, camouflaging the grazing elk. I wait for them to lift their heads, for Longs Peak to emerge from the early morning mist.

I picture myself in the doorway of our cabin in the fall of 1966, my sophomore year in high school, when my sister does not come home from college. The phone rings long after my bedtime. It's the campus police. They found Alice outside a fraternity house, wandering around in her nightgown, babbling about her fiancé, the Olympic runner Jim Ryun, whom she had been stalking for weeks.

"She has never met Jim Ryun," Mother says.

They take her to Menninger psychiatric hospital in Topeka. After weeks of testing and observations, the doctors are unanimous in their diagnosis: schizophrenia.

I have no idea what this means. I only know that Alice is not coming home anytime soon and that there is one less table setting for Christmas dinner. The platter of sliced roast turkey and bowls of gravy and mashed potatoes pass from Mother at the head of the table, to my grandparents, to Dad, to me. We bow our heads as Dad says grace, Alice's name and whereabouts unmentioned. Then we eat in silence, Grandmother in no mood to hum her favorite Christmas carol in between mouthfuls of food.

Three years later I leave home for good, having rejected offers from three liberal arts schools on the East Coast in favor of my first choice. Colorado College is the last to notify me. My parents are relieved. I will earn the degree Alice never will, in the protective embrace of Pikes Peak, the first and only college graduate in my family.

4

Serious Moves

Karl makes the first move when he stops by my desk during his lunch break. "Cute dress," he says. The opposite of what my boss had to say about my sleeveless pink and lime-green Hawaiian muumuu.

I welcome the interruption. Typing and retyping computer hardware specifications and price quotation requests isn't what I envisioned as a recently graduated history major.

Those stark green eyes. A feature that nails me to my chair, leaving me breathless. They cut right through his wire-rim glasses and defeat whatever resistance might arise in the face of certain facts had they been known. His girlfriend in California, for instance, whom he fails to mention. The difference in age. Maybe neither of these complications would have knocked him out of contention. His thick, curly beard, barrel chest, and big, hairy hands, rather than intimidating me, epitomize my conception of a mountain man.

Our first date Karl picks me up in his Ford Bronco for the drive to the Mount Sherman trailhead. There are fifty-four mountains in the Colorado Rockies that are over fourteen thousand feet high. Karl wants to climb them all—the conquest, by his reckoning, to be completed within a couple of summers. According to the Colorado Mountain Club guidebook, Mount Sherman (the Sherman who helped win the Civil War with his scorched-earth strategy) is one of the easiest fourteeners, a romp through the tundra and an ideal introduction to mountaineering.

I do not question Karl's choice of hiking mates or the timing of our departure. He is ten years older, with two master's degrees from

Stanford. At two months old, he rode to the top of a peak overlooking Los Angeles in his father's backpack. At eleven he made it to the top of Mount Whitney, the highest mountain in the Lower 48, on his own two feet—his nausea from the altitude tempered by the view his father indicated with a sweep of his arm. In college, a summer of scrambling up the tourist-free routes of Mount Moran and the Grand in Teton National Park assured Karl's rite of passage to manhood.

I come from more sedentary stock. My parents admired the view of Longs Peak from our cabin in Rocky Mountain National Park. At home in Kansas City my mother kept in shape, and her hair dry, by dogpaddling at the country club pool in her shower cap, while my father traversed the golf course in a motorized cart, knocking off eight or nine holes of golf without breaking a sweat. During tornado drills in elementary school I could duck and roll with the best of them, but the vertical drop from wooden seat to linoleum floor barely exceeded two feet, not enough conditioning for the physical challenges of mountaineering.

On Mount Sherman, Karl and I are the only ones going up. Everyone else is coming down. They started hiking at daybreak; we arrived at the trailhead at noon. They stick to the well-established trail; Karl improvises a shortcut. I manage to stay within earshot until we reach timberline and Karl catches his second wind. The rougher and steeper the terrain, the more impressive his performance. Boulders that remain upright as he hops from one to the next lurch and buck me off. He gains altitude; a landslide carries me backward in slow motion, toward the Bronco. At this rate Karl will bag the summit before I can scramble to my feet. The wind doesn't help; its velocity pummels me, pinning me in place.

The wind drags a sheet of moisture in its wake, draping our destination in gray. The ferocity of the impending storm is telegraphed with a buzz of electricity. The subsequent boom sounds like it has blown up the ridge, and the echo roars across the basin. Spared from the humiliation of failure by a lightning bolt. I did not see the flash of light that preceded the strike, but Karl must have. He is running down the boulder field, the boulders rolling and rocking beneath his dancing feet. Force of will harnessing force of gravity. Wobbling and spinning, he remains upright as ball after ball whirls beneath him for the strike.

After that outing we cast ourselves as Lord Alfred and Lady Emily in a Gothic adventure story inspired by my maternal English ancestry and favorite novelist in adolescence.

"Alfred!" I shout whenever I lose sight of him, which is frequently.

"Emily, over here," identifying his location with a wave of his white sailor's hat.

He tries to let down the California girlfriend gently. She wants to know why. He says I don't mind sleeping in the back of the Bronco with the tailgate open so we can watch for shooting stars, and I contain my hysteria when his unconventional route up Mount Banca peters out, and we have to turn around and descend the same steep, icy couloir we crawled up. Karl left the rope in the Bronco.

His bouquet of roses for my birthday is a photo of Lady Emily stretched out on a hummock of Rocky Mountain sedge and Arctic gentian. His Christmas card is a photo of a blue spruce in a twinkling coat of fresh snow. We didn't make that summit. We lost our traction in the windblown drifts.

Karl makes the next move atop Mount Elbert, the highest mountain in the state. Above timberline I am still a virgin. He advances with the certitude of a bull elk that just defeated its primary opponent, pants shoved below hips, buttons on shirt yielding to dizzy fingers. We toss our clothing in a reckless heap and kneel on our jackets—lips, tongues, fingers probing as dusk circles, cutting off our escape route. Semi-oblivious, we weave together and apart in a serpentine tango choreographed by the same forces that drive the speeding clouds overhead. A Peeping Tom of a marmot whistles for handouts. Rocked by laughter, our knees buckle and we collapse, Bull Elk on top. My spine is paralyzed against stone. Bull Elk consummates the coupling as the sun crashes into a distant ridge, setting the clouds ablaze.

By Christmas, I will think of this sunset as a funeral pyre for my sexual desire, hypnotic and uncontainable, the ashes smoldering long after the flames are spent.

5

Pinned

I'm muddling through my first semester of teaching eighth graders, my idealism and inexperience inadequate to their endlessly creative pranks and twisted jokes, such as the shit the police chief's son leaves on my desk in a brown lunch sack. Christmas break and a quick trip to Kansas City can't come soon enough. My next-door neighbor strings her giant blue spruce in red lights as if celebrating with me. Ten more days. My rented cottage in Cheyenne Canyon, as close to Pikes Peak as I can afford on a temporary teacher's salary, will be secure. My neighbor volunteers to watch over it while I'm gone.

It is five thirty in the morning when my mattress rocks me out of a sound and dreamless sleep. Unlike in Karl's native California, the earth never shakes in Colorado Springs. Maybe I am dreaming. A zombie-eyed, bespectacled creature crouches at the bottom of my bed. The name on his U.S. army tunic is covered in masking tape. His combat boots are scuffed. He doesn't bother to remove them. A bent knee lunges, then its mate. My legs are pinned. A hand seizes my wrists, locking them in an unbreakable grip. The tip of the knife in his other hand presses into my Adam's apple. I can still breathe—barely. This is no dream.

"Do not resist. Do not scream. Or I'll slash your throat."

He doesn't have to threaten me. My throat is incapacitated. I can't make a sound.

"Close your eyes and roll over." He doesn't have to whisper, to muffle his voice. My neighbor is sixty and hard of hearing. Her cottage is on the other side of the parking lot, behind the blue spruce. Her kitchen light won't switch on until seven o'clock. Her shift at the nursing home doesn't start until eight thirty. Roll call begins at six fifteen sharp. He can make it with time to spare. Fort Carson is just fifteen minutes away.

Even if my neighbor were up and I could cry out and she had exceptional hearing, my screams would be muted by sizzling bacon or running water. I wish I could scream because I do not want to die, in my own bed in my first home of my own. I have voted in one presidential election. Paid off the loan for my first car. My suitcase is packed with Christmas presents for my family. The two-week break will do wonders for my morale.

His grip on the knife unrelenting, he straddles my thighs.

"Please, just leave. I won't tell a soul."

"Do what I say and I won't harm you."

"Why me? My purse is on the dresser. Take my money and hire a prostitute."

"Roll over."

My face buried in my pillow, I gasp for what may be my last breath of air. A slight breeze travels up my torso as my nightgown is lifted to my neck. He's going to strangle me with Karl's birthday present. He takes off my underpants and slips them over my head. He'll smother me with my underpants. He turns me over. The stench of dirty underpants fills my nostrils. I hold my breath. He keeps his promise, but the stain he leaves on my belly marks me for life.

I'm shaking uncontrollably. It doesn't occur to me to ask for a blanket. I drove myself to the emergency room without registering a single, mundane detail. Not the scarcity of traffic at such an early hour on a Friday morning. Nor the sensation of my hands on the steering wheel, or foot as it alternated between accelerator and brake pedal.

Accelerating and braking: my state of mind since fleeing my cottage and pounding on my neighbor's door, the giddy red Christmas lights of last night subdued by an overcast dawn.

It must have been cold as I climbed into the driver's seat. That would explain the chattering of my teeth as I sit on the edge of the table. I must have obeyed the speed limit. The police officer who entered the waiting room as I left it is the same police officer who followed me from room to room, notebook in hand, pen in shirt pocket, as I showed him the open drawer with tousled lingerie, the open window with broken latch and missing screen, the paring knife far removed from its customary place on the kitchen counter.

"There must be fingerprints on the window glass and the knife handle," I suggested. He didn't respond. He didn't take any notes either, explaining, "You must be examined by a doctor."

"You can request your own doctor," the ER nurse says, drawing the curtain shut to reassure me that our conversation is confidential. "Some women prefer a doctor they know."

She offers to make the phone call. I must have nodded my head.

She hands me a gown. "It will keep you warm after you undress."

She shuts the curtain behind her when she leaves. Shadows dart back and forth, voices blurring with instruments and rolling stretchers. My mind, when it isn't choking on its own exhaust, races with suppositions. Someone having a heart attack? My doctor approaching?

I am alone in the cubicle. There is nowhere to hide. Shut, the white curtain shields me in a counterfeit veil of privacy. The shadows must have eyes and ears. If I am invisible, it's because of the glare of the overhead fluorescent light. My yellow flannel nightgown, Karl's birthday present, slips off easily, discarded like a soiled diaper, never to be worn or touched again. I cover myself as best I can with the gown. Disposable. Antiseptic white like the tissue beneath me, the color scheme of the entire emergency room.

I curl up in a ball, a position that exposes my buttocks and thighs to the blinding interrogation of the overhead fluorescent light. I can't stop shivering; my hands and feet are numb even though the tissue is dissolving in a pool of sweat, affixing my buttocks to the vinyl pad underneath.

Three men in green caps and gowns slip in unnoticed, the purpose of their visit unknown until they are standing at the foot of the table, snickering at the cleverness of their jokes. For the first time in my life, I'm grateful for my inability to remember a punch line. The nurse pokes her head in and hollers, "Out!" A command they obey. Then, more gently, she addresses me. "Your doctor is running late."

9:10 A.M., 9:17 A.M., 9:31 A.M. The minute hand on the clock divorces itself from linear time. 10:09 A.M., 10:38. I am a corpse on a stainless-steel table, its departing soul observing the autopsy from an impartial distance.

10:55, 11:22, 11:49. The hands on the clock join in prayer. Several minutes later the curtain parts and my doctor strides in, all three orderlies in tow. He looks as old as my father, only slimmer glasses and waistline, brusque demeanor, all business. He has patients at his office with appointments, he says, and he mustn't keep them waiting, so he dispenses with the introductions and sets the cubicle in motion with a string of barked orders. A sheet is draped over my pelvis. My legs extend, the scene of the crime submitting to the mandatory examination.

"Scoot closer," the doctor says, the orderlies peering over his shoulders.

"Slide hips toward stirrups." *Please do not repeat that command.* Doctor incapable of reading lips. At first pinch of stainless steel, heels withdraw from stirrups; gloved hands take over, latex squealing as it contacts skin.

Afterward, the conversation recedes to the other side of the curtain, where it is conducted in silhouetted mime. Two heads. One bobbing, the other leaning in, foreheads practically touching. Someone is mumbling something indecipherable, as if to ensure no eavesdropping. The bulging outline of a holstered gun betrays the speaker's identity. The volume rises. My doctor is weighing in. He tells the police officer, "I can't be certain. She isn't a virgin."

Not a virgin. Words my mother, and other women of her generation, might have used to frighten their daughters into chastity for an unforgiving marital marketplace.

The squeak of rubber soles traverses marble. Not one ripple disturbs the curtain. I sit up so I can determine the direction of the footsteps. The police officer is not as light on his feet as the soldier. He is vacating the scene of the second crime without consulting the victim.

I slept with my boyfriend by choice. The soldier who pried open the window with a screwdriver coerced my consent with a knife. If they do not believe me, there will be more victims. If they do not believe me, I'll have to give up my cottage and disappear.

"I'll kill you if you tell," my rapist whispered when he was done. Maybe he was bluffing because of the uniform I had glimpsed before he covered my head with my underpants. Prior experience must have taught him the value of stealth. His next destination insinuated not by footsteps, but creaking floorboards until they, too, fell silent. He must have left by the front door. My heart thumped with deafening ambiguity. Then it exploded in my ears like a shotgun blast. I could hear his breath in the doorway to my bedroom. He promised he wouldn't hurt me if I complied. I kept my end of the bargain. Why couldn't he?

Now he has a good reason to kill me. I told.

Next morning, I go door to door, with notebook and pen, studying the eyewear and haircut of every man in the neighborhood who answers my knocks. I will solve this crime myself. A friend calls to check on me. "Are you crazy? He's bound to recognize you."

I meet with an investigative reporter, who publishes a front-page series about the number of uninvestigated, unprosecuted rape cases in the county. His sources remain anonymous to protect us from retaliation but also the shame.

Greg, a new friend, stops calling after the police interrogation. He is incensed. Although the length of his hair and his pronounced limp fail to match my description of the rapist, the detective seems more interested in pursuing a line of inquiry that will confirm his suspicions of me than following up leads that will result in an arrest.

A soldier from Fort Carson? He might be a decorated vet, who muddied his boots in the stinking, sweltering, booby-trapped jungles of Cu Chi and put his puckered ass on the line to defend South Vietnam, and by extension the rest of Southeast Asia, from communism. If Saigon falls, Phnom Penh and Bangkok will topple, and the red menace will infiltrate Kuala Lumpur, Jakarta, and Tokyo.

For women in my position, the domino theory works in reverse. I have been taken by surprise, in my own bed, the assault and its collateral damage unverified by a third party and therefore dubious. Having violated the morality code and tainted her testimony with her prior sexual history, the only witness has compromised her standing in the court of public opinion. Her body has already been invaded and occupied, so there is no honor left to defend.

The compliant, malleable heroines in the romance novels of my adolescence trap me in a narrative as old as Adam and Eve. The character assigned to me, a Bronze Age archetype, overwhelms my barely formed sense of me. Who am I, a twenty-four-year-old neophyte in a recessionary job market and with few marital prospects, to question the authorities, to assert a contrary point of view? The Texas Rangers and the cheerleaders made the rules clear. The punishment for deviation is ridicule and rejection. The vocabulary for a more sympathetic and accurate interpretation of my experience doesn't exist yet. I must become fluent in a foreign tongue before I can translate my experience into a comprehensible language: The soldier is a thief. He has stolen my right to self-determination and governance; he has broken into and entered my body and taken what I, and I alone, have the authority to give. Am I not the property owner in this case? But no lock has been jimmied, no contents visibly removed, no outward harm done to bolster my claim.

Karl believes me. The only one. On temporary assignment in California, he calls every night after work, checking on the progress of the investigation. My mother, wondering how on earth I will support myself in the years to come, is encouraged by his devotion.

I do not tell them where I really sleep—on sofas in friends' apartments—until I wear out their welcome and relocate for the night to the back of my Volkswagen hatchback. After supper I pack up my sleeping bag and toiletries and drive up the canyon to the parking lot of a four-star hotel overlooked by Cheyenne Mountain. The security lights in the parking lot relieve the anxiety of chronic insomnia. Wherever I bed down for the night, I sleep fitfully, so I might as well sleep within shouting range of a security guard. He may be gray-haired and unarmed, but the beam of his flashlight might intimidate felons taking advantage of the dark.

Although I never sleep there, I keep my cottage. I can't bear to give up the home Karl transformed with his voluntary labor before departing for California. He pulled up the filthy, worn carpet, tossed it into the back of his Bronco, hauled it off to the dump; sanded and restained the pine floor underneath. A whiff of nostalgia for Bowen Woods engulfed me. With two coats of sunflower yellow he brightened the dingy walls in the living room. It took a while to adjust to the avocado green he selected for my bedroom. The similarity to a mental hospital ward unnerved me at first. My appreciation for his taste grew in his absence. The color lulled me to sleep as I pined for the down comforter of his warm, furry skin.

How does one reclaim a disintegrating human being? My mind won't give me a moment's rest. The filth cannot be swept away, shaken off. It's too contaminated for the dump. The mere sight of avocado green freezes me in an instant replay of a knife-wielding soldier kneeling on my thighs, of three amused orderlies inspecting the scene of the crime.

Unlike my neighbor and Greg—"Why didn't you scream? Fight back?"—Karl assigns no blame. I was raped. How could anyone pass judgment or doubt my credibility? I wish his confidence would rub off on me. Home is a place, a state of mind, a relationship with my body. I have lost faith in all three.

On his return from California, Karl drives a row of nails into the complicit window sash. "I should have done this before I left," he mutters. "Nailed it half shut." To test the strength of the nails, he shoves the window up as far as he can. "There," he says. "The son of a bitch would have to be a midget in a Styrofoam suit to survive the broken glass. As deadly as shrapnel."

We set the wedding date for July, at the peak of the wildflower season, when the blooming meadows are aflutter with nectar-seeking painted ladies. The ceremony takes place in an outdoor chapel overlooking Cripple Creek and its cemetery, where death is the great equalizer, and gunslingers and prostitutes have been laid to rest alongside respectable mining families. When the minister finishes his recitation and turns to me, my mind goes blank. I can't remember my part of the agreement, even though I wrote the vows. The ring Karl slips on my finger is set in agate. He purchased the polished stone at a rock shop after noting the resemblance to the color of my eyes. I string the necklace I made of leather and wooden beads around his neck. After the ceremony a friend of my father's says, "You looked like the hangman at an execution, Jane."

6

Roped

We will be safe here atop our forested cliff in the shadow of Pikes Peak. Seventy-two steps buffer the skinny front yard from the street below. I count the steps my first trip down. The gate at the bottom is rusted shut. If that doesn't discourage the curious, the tunnel of interlocking branches of overgrown lilac and rose bushes above the gate will. Near the top, blue spruce and scrub oak lean over a cliff, ready to launch at the slightest disturbance. A trespasser might die in this Mad Hatter's tea party of foliage.

I concur with Karl's decision. After months of searching, he has finally found the perfect property: one of the biggest, oldest homes in Manitou Springs, on five steep acres abutting a national forest.

We park the Bronco in the lot above the house and follow the realtor down the crumbling steps. "Now is the time to buy fixer-uppers," he says. "This house has potential."

Karl hopes the bank will agree. In 1976 few banks loan money for homes in Manitou Springs; lenders associate the historic renovation market with hippies who skip town after the marijuana bust.

The location keeps the frantic city at arm's length and the mountainside above within a moment's reach. Our dog can roam to his heart's content without being hit by a car. We can escape whenever we wish, throw open the back door and walk up into the sunlight and scarlet paintbrush. Eventually the forest will envelop us, dampening the clamor of buzzing saws and backfiring mufflers. The forest goes on and on, obliterating the sounds of human activity, splintering the sun into a fractured glow. We can hike all the way to Cripple Creek on the other side of Pikes Peak, in solitude punctuated by chattering pine jays.

"This house has character," Karl says as he gazes up at the ivy-lined walkway to the faded redwood deck on the second story. A windowless addition to the rear end of the house covers the original core, constructed in 1886, and we have to walk inside to see the Victorian details: windows framed in rippled, multicolored stained glass; soaring ceilings; a locally quarried stone fireplace the color of rain and sagebrush; picture-rail Douglas fir moldings for hanging Karl's nature photos.

From the veranda on the front of the house, we can hear the gushing of the creek below. I picture us in wicker chairs, Karl in his white wedding tuxedo, me in my silk gown with off-white lace trim, sipping strawberry daiquiris, our laughter the toast of the town. We will grow old here together; when our spines can no longer endure the wicker furniture, we will replace it with a hammock and cushioned rocking chair, and doze away the afternoon, reminiscing about all the mountains we climbed in our carefree youth.

In the master bedroom upstairs, I can raise the window, step out on the balcony, and spy on the neighbors on the other side of the canyon, provided I tread lightly on the rotten floor joists. The hillside opposite is choked with lopsided dwellings and corkscrewed alleys that serve as streets. A castle, built for a French priest in 1896 and converted into apartments after the war, is surrounded by bungalows, cottages, and wannabe mansions whose original owners were rather careless in their haste to escape civilization or tuberculosis or the disappointment of a failed relationship. There are too many structures for one eroding hillside to bear, and a century after the building boom, survival seems questionable. How much longer will the houses stay put on those sagging foundations and tilted streets? Perhaps the priest, who abandoned his castle within three years of moving in, was uneasy about the precariousness of the location.

We don't notice the precariousness of our location until after the loan is approved and Karl has signed the mortgage papers and made the down payment.

Karl calls the house Ruxton House, for his hero, the peripatetic Englishman George Frederick Ruxton, who spent the winter of 1847 exploring the Colorado Rockies. The canyon and street below are named for him. After his expulsion from Sandhurst military academy at age fifteen and a short-lived career as a mercenary in Europe and Canada, he abandoned the profession of his paternal ancestors and struck out for the frontier. Africa first, and when that continent proved too difficult to explore, the American West, where a competent outdoorsman could live like James Fenimore Cooper's Leatherstocking.

Camped near one of the half-dozen springs in the canyon, Ruxton was convinced he had found the idyllic spot to winter; the hibernating grizzlies were too wary to pose a serious threat, and the elk, antelope, and buffalo grazed nonchalantly in plain sight, fulfilling the promise of Cooper's ecstatic prose. Black-tailed deer filed by like revolving wooden ducks at a shooting gallery. Sheep, Ruxton called them, and he wasn't being derogatory. Unlike the beaver trappers, whose indiscriminate slaughter he disliked, Ruxton questioned his own zealotry. They came to him as if he had whistled in a loyal hunting dog, and watched, tails quivering, as he shot the plumpest buck in the heart. The band scattered and the buck took off with them on convulsing legs until it stopped and ran around in circles. As suddenly as it bolted, it toppled over.

I prefer the original name of the house, the Bird Cage, Miss Ida Clothier's boarding school for girls. The true nature of her business was more profitable. Local politicos who were regular customers saw to it that she didn't have to pay property taxes. Miss Clothier's girls also serviced the miners who rode the narrow-gauge train to Cripple Creek and back. The tracks were pulled up after World War II, but the railroad bed still parallels the upper property line, and Tunnel Number 2 remains standing and undisturbed except for the hoots of the owl nesting in the decomposing eaves.

Inside the house and out, the passage of time shows—the chandeliers removed by subsequent owners, as well as anything else of value that could be pried loose and sold. Miss Clothier's gold and chartreuse exterior color scheme painted over in respectable white; the pink bedrooms, in psych-ward green. The yard, all five vertical acres of it, left to nature.

There are cracks in the walls and missing shingles and other defects, but as the realtor said, this house has potential. Whatever doubts I have, I keep to myself. I don't want to upset the balance of power any more than it already is. Karl picked the property and Karl paid for it. My name was left off the title because I had nothing to contribute to the transaction.

Karl calls the defects "projects." The leaking pipes, pinstriped plywood paneling, peeling wallpaper, and crumbling lath and plaster, false ceilings and converted coal-fired furnace, which wastes more energy than it produces, can be repaired or replaced. The number and complexity of projects appeal to the engineer in him.

Despite the demands of his engineering projects at work and at home, Karl also makes the decorating decisions. It is easier to let him win than to hold my own in a debate with a Stanford man who contributes ten times the income to the household budget than I can with my occasional substitute teaching gigs in a saturated profession.

The antique cathouse sofa in the living room is mine, even though he paid for it. It is his birthday gift. Reupholstered in burgundy velvet and with new springs, it will support the weight of my ambition—to be as alluring as the dance hall girls of Cripple Creek, who assembled in the Imperial Hotel lobby in their satin and silk finery to advertise their wares in hopes of attracting a gold miner who hadn't gambled his money away.

Weekdays, Karl's job and voluntary community service frequently engage him until bedtime. Perhaps he is beginning to notice my absence in bed. My mind associates arousal with consent, regardless of the circumstances. Unable to distinguish between the arousal of terror and the arousal of genuine desire, my body will respond and participate—as long as my mind preoccupies itself elsewhere. The man who strokes my hair isn't Karl, but an imaginary lover I seduced in a low-cut, red satin gown and white pearls. I can't believe my good fortune. Of all the gold miners prospecting for sex in Cripple Creek, he is the kindest and most attentive. Blond with blue eyes, the color of my dad's. His caresses and compliments more real to me than the scratching of Karl's whiskers on my cheek, the tickle of his breath in my ear.

A shiver of fear courses through me, setting my skin on edge. Is this how Alice's mind unraveled, one imperceptible thread at a time?

I recover my equilibrium on weekends. After three summers with Karl as my mountaineering guide, I can almost keep up. No more cramped calves or searing headaches from oxygen and water deprivation or mandatory rest steps to catch my breath. Soft, shapeless muscle has toughened up, rounded out. Legs and lungs perform in harmony, powering me up the mountain.

The pikas have instructed me well in the art of surviving in inhospitable environments. A cousin of the rabbit and one of the few mammals to risk winter above timberline, it adapted by sacrificing its big ears and bushy tail for heat conservation. What must I sacrifice for Karl and me to meet our peak-bagging objectives, for our union to gratify us both? We collect summits with the frenzied purposefulness of the pikas in their quest for enough food to outlast winter. In their race against extinction, they waste not one second. Layer upon layer of dried sedges, thistles, and grasses, the haystacks rise, grandiose as the pyramids of the Aztecs.

7

Souljourners

I have a husband who supports me, a defensible home on a mountain-side, a national forest in my backyard. Yet a hazy discontent casts a pall over my days, incurable for lack of a proper diagnosis. Perhaps my maternal ancestry predisposes me to flights of unhappiness. The English are a nomadic breed. The dreary weather and insufferable class hierarchy might have driven them mad otherwise. George Ruxton wasn't the only nineteenth-century Englishman who fled to the remote frontier. He wrote, "I must confess the very happiest moments of my life have been spent in the wilderness of the Far West; and I never recall but with pleasure my solitary camp with no friend near me more faithful than my rifle, and no companions more sociable than my good horse and mules, or the attendant cayute which nightly serenaded us. . . . Scarcely, however, did I ever wish to change such hours of freedom for all the luxuries of civilized life."

With little to do during mud season but plot next summer's hiking misadventures, I am a housebound voyeur in need of inspiration—a guidebook perhaps to the terra incognita of my interior. Isabella Bird's fifth book, *A Lady's Life in the Rocky Mountains*, seldom out of print since its publication in 1879, offers a woman's perspective from an earlier time that might illuminate the source of my malaise. The cover illustration for one edition depicts a youthful redhead riding a horse in a peach gown and matching bonnet—a sugary confection bearing no resemblance to the actual Isabella.

My first trip to Colorado, in the summer of 1954, at age three, I arrived atop the portable toilet in the back of our Ford woody, pointing at the

Brown Palace Hotel and screeching, "Lookee! Lookee!" as we tunneled through the tightfisted streets of downtown Denver. On her first and only trip to Colorado, in the fall of 1873, Isabella Bird took the train from Cheyenne, Wyoming, to Greeley, marveling, as she noted in her journal, at the mountains that "upheave themselves above the prairie seas. Gradually they are gaining possession of me. I can look at, and feel, nothing else."

The Colorado frontier provided few amenities for tourists, especially the rare female tourist. By wagon, Isabella traveled from Greeley to Fort Collins, two godforsaken, bug-ridden, money-mad settlements on the dusty, rattlesnake-infested plains, fortifying her resolve to reach the tranquil mountain valley of Estes Park. The closer she got, the more irresistible her destination. When she finally arrived at the village of Longmont, one mountain prevailed over the forested foothills: "the splintered, pinnacled, lonely, ghastly, imposing summit of Longs Peak, the Mont Blanc of northern Colorado."

The Isabella Bird I meet in the pages of her book and surviving letters to her only sibling speaks to the paradoxes in my life. There are two Isabellas: the despairing invalid beset with fevers, backaches, boils, and nervousness, and the intrepid adventuress of steely fortitude. Some of her ailments were medically induced, others the result of poor hygiene. But loss contributed, too, such as the death in 1858 of her father, an Evangelical clergyman, and the death of her mother eight years later. Abroad, Isabella suffered few of the maladies that left her bedridden, and her doctors mystified, at home. In Hawaii, the first leg of her 1873 trip, she wrote her sister, Henrietta, "I did wild things I cannot do with white people, such as galloping up and down hills, halloing my horse to go faster, . . . riding without stirrups and other free and easy ways. I thought of nothing all that day." In the California Sierras she parted company with her horse when a grizzly rose up out of the brush, growling. She dusted herself off and walked for nearly an hour, until she met up with the wagoner dispatched to find her.

Her doctors could not find a cure because they were unable to diagnose the primary, underlying cause of her condition. A well-bred Christian

woman was supposed to derive satisfaction from self-sacrifice and charitable deeds. If she failed to secure a suitable husband, she lived with her
parents, their helpmate until their death; then she moved in with relatives
and tended their household and children. She didn't go to school. The
rare school for girls groomed its charges for marriage and domestic
martyrdom. Universities excluded women. So Isabella was schooled at
home. Her mother tutored her in the Bible, history, and literature; her
father taught her Latin and botany.

Her first attempt to reach Estes Park was thwarted by a snowstorm
and an incompetent guide. Her innkeeper in Longmont recruited better
guides once his skepticism was satisfied. An unchaperoned English-
woman riding a rented horse in an ankle-length skirt and bloomers? The
two young men, recent arrivals in Colorado themselves, tried to conceal
their disappointment. They had hoped to escort a young, vivacious
beauty, not one plump with middle age.

Not only was Isabella traveling alone, in defiance of the conventions
of Victorian society, she was a forty-one-year-old spinster who had
rejected a variety of suitors at home and abroad. Dr. Bishop, her sister's
physician, was kind, well spoken, and steadfast—admirable traits in a
friend but exceedingly dull in a husband. The farmer Mr. Wilson, the
Canadian immigrant she met in Australia, overreached himself. She
forgave him, attributing his gaffe to ignorance of her social position.
Colonel Heath deserved her fierce rejection for he should have known
better. A veteran of the Confederate army proposing to a descendant of
outspoken abolitionists? The nerve!

Not that she minded the attention. With the exception of Colonel
Heath, she sought the company of adventurous men who would escort
her into forbidden territory for women of her station.

In Colorado, Isabella's guides did not disappoint. September 28, 1873:
"I have just dropped into the very place I have been seeking, but in
everything it exceeds all my dreams. There is health in every breath of
air. . . . I have a log cabin . . . all to myself."

A warm bed out of the wind—what more do I need? For all of its partially realized charms, Ruxton House feels unnecessarily cavernous in comparison to the snug simplicity of our cabin at Bowen Woods, Alice asleep beside me, the window latched, a pile of blankets warding off the night chill. She sleeps soundly, perhaps lost in the enchanted forest of her dreams, as the wind knocks on the window and pine needles ping the glass. The monsters biding their time as Alice ventures farther into the woods and I run after her. Hers will be a half-life, the rate of decay accelerating as adulthood nears. A life is not worth stealing until its promise becomes evident. In high school her mastery of French will impress her teacher, a native speaker. Her drawings will display a talent for fashion design. She will invite me along on outings with her boyfriend. Me in the back seat, the unacknowledged chaperone and comedian providing an entertaining diversion. Mother cautioned us. Men may expect things we shouldn't give. Some are downright dangerous.

The shock of his appearance nearly dismounted Isabella. There was only one trail to Griff Evan's summer ranch in Estes Park, and it passed by the hut of the infamous squatter, Jim Nugent, better known as Rocky Mountain Jim. The paws of a beaver pelt dangled from his saddle. A digger's scarf held up his deerskin pants. A knife was stuck in his belt and a revolver bulged out of his breast pocket. A grizzly had ravaged one eye. He turned his head, revealing the perfection of his profile, and spoke. She was astonished. Such refinement. His conduct unimpeachable. A true gentleman.

But that face: one half scarred beyond human, lending credence to his self-portrayal as the most notorious desperado in the Rocky Mountain West, his crimes too horrific for a genteel woman like Isabella to bear in detail. The other half, worthy of imitation in marble and befitting the poetry he recited in a soft Irish brogue. Many of the verses she knew. Others had the ring of romanticized bravado.

In conversation and rhyme, he recounted his former life—more like nine lives—as a scout on the plains, a renegade soldier in the Indian Wars, an outlaw. Perhaps Isabella fleshed out the titillating details at night, alone in her cabin, huddled beneath a pile of blankets as the wind whistled through the chinks and the wolves howled and a grizzly sniffed for an unprotected calf. Whose version was more spellbinding? The Rocky Mountain Jim of his invention? Or the Rocky Mountain Jim of her imagination that set tongues wagging about their relationship after the publication of *A Lady's Life in the Rocky Mountains*?

He was born in Canada of Irish parents and left home at eighteen, determined to make a clean break from his troubled family and an unrequited infatuation. The rest of his biography varied from storyteller to storyteller. A visiting Englishman nicknamed Rocky Mountain Jim "the Mountainous One" for the "the extraordinary altitude of his lies." He was a Canadian all right, though not necessarily an admirable one. Rumor had it that he was a defrocked priest or a disgraced school teacher, maybe both.

He had settled in Estes Park five years before Isabella's arrival, one of a handful of squatters on the run from the tyrannical claims of human society. Between his fur trapping and his hunting, he knew this country as well as anyone: the elk and Indian trails, the best places to trap beaver and watch a sunset. In this man of culture and child of nature, as Isabella described him, she saw her own reflection.

Three weeks before Isabella's arrival, newspapers from Greeley to Denver had trumpeted the triumph of Anna Dickinson. "The spice, the pepper and the brains" of the women's suffragist movement, as one reporter put it, had summited Longs Peak, first woman ever. In the absence of evidence to the contrary, the claim, though mistaken, was accepted as fact.

After learning of Dickinson's achievement, Isabella wouldn't leave Estes Park until she summited Longs Peak herself. In Hawaii she had slept on the rim of Mauna Loa's fire-breathing caldera, nearly fourteen thousand feet above the sea, an outing so exhilarating she was reluctant to leave the islands.

Griff Evans, Dickinson's guide, tried to dissuade Isabella. *October is no month to indulge in an alpine expedition, and you can't ride a horse to the top of the mountain.* The weather turned unseasonably warm and dry. Reassured, Evans loaned her some hunting boots. Her boots were falling apart. Rocky Mountain Jim would be her guide—she insisted on it—and the two young men who accompanied her to Estes would join them in hopes of also making the summit.

October 1873: "We rode upwards through the gloom on a steep trail blazed through forest, all my intellect concentrated on avoiding being dragged off my horse by impending branches.... The gloom of the dense, ancient, silent forest is to me awe-inspiring. . . . it is soundless, except for the branches creaking in the soft wind, the frequent snap of decayed timber, and a murmur in the pine tops as of a not distant waterfall, all tending to produce eeriness and a sadness hardly akin to pain."

They camped in the nearest grove to timberline. Before retiring for the night, they sang their favorite songs by the campfire, the volume of their voices drowning out the howls of the wolves. Jim recited one more poem, of his own composition. The fair maiden was Griff Evan's teenage daughter.

From her bed of pine boughs and borrowed blankets, Isabella studied Jim's sleeping face. The untouched half was turned toward her. Closed, his ravaged eye lost its frightful association with the legendary encounter with a grizzly in Middle Park.

October 1976: It is a three-and-a-half-hour drive from Ruxton House to the trailhead parking lot for Longs Peak. We set out at noon, hours later than the hikers who will complete the ascent in one day. Karl carries the backpack with his provisions, the stove and matches, tarp, and both sleeping bags. I carry a daypack with my rain gear, lunch, and canteen. The sun beats down on us as we trudge up the endless, eroded switchbacks through the forest. Perspiring every step of the way, I relinquish more moisture than my canteen can replenish. The forest gradually peters out, giving way to rocky tundra. Blisters burn the bottoms of my feet. Although it means we will be pitching the tarp in the dark, I am grateful for the onset of dusk until I start shivering in my damp shirt. When we reach our designated campsite in Jim's Grove, where Isabella and Rocky Mountain Jim camped, we are too tired to rekindle their unconsummated romance. In a burst of crimson the sun flares out of sight. Thinned for firewood over the years, Jim's Grove provides scant shelter from the wind.

They departed after breakfast, the men walking while Isabella rode. They hobbled her horse at the bottom of a shattered expanse of boulders slickened by a recent snowstorm. From here, they would have to continue on foot. Griff Evans's boots were too big, and Isabella repeatedly slipped and fell. She found a better-fitting pair behind a rock, probably left by Anna Dickinson. The shoes fit. But even with the best of gear, the icy, shifting rocks would have hindered their progress. As they gained elevation, their lungs ached from lack of oxygen, their throats throbbed from lack of water.

Jim carried a rope. Pulling her by the arms and the rope around her waist, he succeeded in getting them both to the notch, where the climb began in earnest. A thousand feet of granite towered above them; one ledge after another had to be surmounted, icier and more exposed than what they had traversed below. Not one step could be trusted.

"My feet were paralyzed," Isabella wrote.

Over her protests, Jim pushed on. Terrified and exhausted, Isabella insisted on returning to the notch. The rest of the party could summit without her.

One of their companions concurred. "A woman is a dangerous encumbrance."

Jim wouldn't stand for it. "If it isn't to take a lady up, I won't go up at all."

To make certain Isabella could continue, Jim explored further until he was turned back by an impassable blockage of ice. On his return he announced his decision. He would descend with Isabella in search of a better approach on the other side of the summit ridge. With the confidence of youth, their companions proceeded with the original plan. Several hundred feet below the summit they waited several hours for Jim and Isabella to rejoin them for the last steep scramble. To Isabella, the granite face Jim hauled her up was "as nearly perpendicular as anything could well be which it was possible to climb." Clinging to the rope, pushed from behind, pulled from above, she jammed her toes and fingers into cracks until her hands gripped one last ledge.

They stood together atop the Continental Divide, atop the highest mountain in the northern Colorado Rockies, gasping for breath as they gazed at stacks of snow-covered peaks, the teardrop aquamarine of lakes, the silver threads of rivers tumbling toward the Atlantic and Pacific Oceans.

Isabella's achievement was tempered with embarrassment. "I have no head and no ankles, and never ought to dream of mountaineering; and had I known that the ascent was a real mountaineering feat I should not have felt the slightest ambition to perform it. As it is, I am only humiliated by my success, for Jim dragged me up, like a bale of goods, by sheer force of muscle."

At dawn we pack up our gear at Jim's Grove and hike into the alpenglow that tints the Diamond rose, then amber. Our slog through the boulder field takes longer than for other parties. My inexperience keeps us at the back of the pack, where we stay because of the slipperiness of the icy rocks. The ice does not melt until we reach the notch beyond which Isabella at first refused to go. Jim persuaded her with the force of his personality and rope. Karl rewards me with a chunk of his favorite chocolate, dark German chocolate that will supposedly revitalize me for the final push. The traverse from the other side of the notch follows a broad ledge, and then the real climb, which so terrified Isabella, begins. In comparison to the boulder field, the rock feels secure as long as I focus on the placement of Karl's hands and feet above me, and not the exposure. But the steepness and oxygen deprivation sap my energy, and Karl has to coax me up with hyperbolic praise and more offerings of chocolate.

On top, I straddle the Continental Divide of my childhood. To the west, partially blocked by a humpbacked, forested ridge, Fred Bowen's meadow registers as a thumbprint on a three-dimensional painting. I see my mother, hands cupped to her eyes, watching for the return of Jane Clark, intrepid explorer. I see what Isabella and Jim saw, stripped of snow: a one hundred and eighty-degree panorama of mountains, their tips practically quivering in the fitful sunlight. To the east, beyond the forested foothills and treeless plateaus of the Front Range, the Euclidean grid of industrialized agriculture and suburbia checkers the grasslands tan and pewter. Along the horizon cultivated prairie merges with sky, the possible border with Kansas vaguely discernible in a dreamlike sheen of dust.

Through the shimmering haze, the past declares itself in waves. I hear the creation story of a mountain range as glaciers grind warped earth into valleys; I hear the report of spent rifles and thunder of stampeding ghost buffalo as soldiers follow in the wake of fur trappers and surveyors; I hear the forbidden chants of captive nomads death-marched onto reservations. I see the saber-toothed tigers and woolly mammoths and Isabella's wolves before they were hunted to extinction; Coronado, greed-stricken and delusional, driving his men to madness; covered wagons bearing my maternal ancestors from Virginia to Ohio to Kansas, that faint blur on the horizon; miners dynamiting for fool's gold that glitters in their hands and dispatches them at an unjust age to cemeteries now covered in weeds and fallen tombstones; the whores of Cripple Creek and Silverton and Central City, who died young and heartbroken, embraced in the afterlife by the high society that spurned them.

When they finally reached camp, the men lifted Isabella off her horse and wrapped her in blankets. The sun had set hours ago. She fell asleep within minutes only to awaken to benumbed feet. Jim was sitting by the fire that illuminated the handsome side of his face. She joined him. He had freed her frock from a rock with his hunting knife, lowered her down with his shoulders—the rope, like her fingers, too stiffened by the damp cold to assist her during the descent from the summit. Now they sat by the fire, Longs Peak white with frost, while Jim wept and spoke of his wasted youth and shattered heart.

At such a high elevation, the stars and constellations Isabella had memorized as a child looked huge. "For five minutes at the camping ground on Longs Peak, I thought love possible." But then she dismissed her feelings as "vanity unpardonable in a woman of forty."

"We will camp at Black Lake. It's only a few hundred feet, I think," Karl says, studying the lake at the head of the valley to the west. Our destination for the night glows obliquely, ominous as a raven's feather, Lake Lady Macbeth. The vertical drop looks like one hundred thousand feet to me. I sit down more often than I stand up, shredding my hiking pants, bruising my butt on the loose rocks.

In the dark we can't find a legal campsite, so Karl guides us by headlamp until he spots an opening in the trees. He ties each end of the tarp to the crossbows of crouching Doug firs, and we crawl under as raindrops the size of silver dollars splash mud. Our tarp leaks; puddles of water soak through our sleeping bags, dividing the down feathers into useless lumps. We hug, absorbing one another's warmth. Karl's lit candle grows fainter as the flame descends. I burrow deeper into the heat of Karl's embrace, studying his expression in the flame, as if by my vigilance both will last the night.

8

Choking

Mother calls. Before hanging up, she manages to choke out a request. "Come home. St. Luke's Hospital is transferring Alice back to her ward at Osawatomie. She refuses to eat, and the staff will have to insert a feeding tube. A feeding tube! They tell me it's a state law." A surgeon repaired the tear in her esophagus from repeatedly stuffing her fingers into her throat and coughing up her undigested meals. If only he could restore her will to live.

Mother calls again, her voice even keeled. "Alice is being transferred to a nursing home. I refuse to let her be force-fed. It's barbaric. Inhumane. I don't care if it's the law, and the staff has to comply. If she wants to die, that's her choice."

I have a faded photo of Alice and me with our cousins—the Texas Rangers—at a birthday party. Whose I do not recall. My front-row grin is worthy of a clown act, highly exaggerated in proportion to the expressions of everyone else, as if I were compensating for Alice's dazed look. She stands apart from the back row, her head turned toward the cracked edge of the photo, her finger pointing at her face as if, having failed to see her reflection in the mirror, she must seek confirmation of her existence elsewhere. On the cusp of adolescence, eight years before her diagnosis, she is tempted to leave, to slip through the looking glass. An adult now, under lock and key for her own safety, she alternates between gulping her food as if it were her last meal on earth and rejecting sustenance altogether. The foreign agent that has colonized her body must be expelled even though it is the voices in her head that conspire against her. Her suffering so irreparable and immense, Mother can't absorb it. I can hear her strangulation over the phone as her sorrowful words catch in her throat.

By the time I get to Kansas City, Alice is confined to a nursing-home bed. Now she gets to decide. A captive of the state, her previous attempts at escape thwarted—from her besieged mind above all—she can starve her way to freedom. Aides scuttle in and out, checking her pulse, her untouched water pitcher. Three days later, they remove an empty tray of food and refill her water pitcher. She must have given up in the night, when no one was watching, the cracked lips, swollen tongue, and cramped legs of severe dehydration too unbearable perhaps to continue the fast. Dad and I meet with the judge while Mother packs up Alice's paltry, threadbare belongings. Something is wrong with the doll Alice tucks under her chin and coos. Twiggy's mouth has fallen off. Mother looks under the bed and in the closet. Her mouth can't be found.

The judge authorizes Alice's return to the state hospital. The staff promises not to force-feed her.

"To think we worried more about you than Alice," Mother confesses. "How wrong we were."

I can no more fish my sister out of the murky depths of mental illness than I can fetch Isabella Bird's papers from the fireplace.

At age seventy-two, her heart failing, Isabella put her affairs in order. A woman without a vocation until middle age, she had published ten books, achieving unimaginable freedom as the principal author of her life. But the slightest variation from the norm brought censure from literary critics, so she crafted her public persona as carefully as her sentences. At her insistence, her book illustrations and photos portray her riding sidesaddle in a skirt, a damned nuisance, even though from Hawaii on, she went native and rode astride like a man, a compromising transgression had she dared to do it at home. Time and again she stepped back from the precipice, tantalizing readers without alienating them. Before her death, letters were burned, passages snipped out, her impeccable sense of public decorum preserved in the afterlife.

With no sister to confide in, I seek an older, wiser surrogate in the passages that survive. Perhaps they will help me navigate the increasingly jumbled terrain of my heart.

After the ascent of Longs Peak, Isabella had a decision to make. With the approach of winter, the snow accumulated, burying the trails and the lakes with a bewildering sameness, until a warm spell would expose the dangerously thin ice over the water. The longer Isabella stayed, the more difficult it would be to leave. If she stayed much longer, she wouldn't get out until spring.

When Jim drank too much whiskey, he cursed and raged at his misspent life and Lord Dunraven's scheme to buy up every acre in the area for a private hunting preserve. Even the roughest of roughnecks avoided him. On their rides into the wilderness, Isabella never knew what to expect: the wit and charm of sobriety, or a drunken fit.

She contemplated going home, but a financial panic had closed the banks, and she was stranded by a shortage of funds until they reopened. So in late October she departed on a six-hundred-mile solo journey through the central Colorado Rockies on horseback, armed with the pistol Jim had loaned her. Perhaps she was seeking another mountainous sanctuary like the one she left behind in Estes Park. Fending for herself, she might forget Rocky Mountain Jim.

On her return to Estes Park, she was horrified by his appearance. He "had grown old and haggard." He paid her a visit at Evans's ranch, two revolvers tucked in his belt, not his customary practice. Several nights later she dreamt he barged into her cabin and shot her.

Her attraction to him confounded her. "I cannot but think of Mr. Wilson in Hawaii and his quiet undemonstrative un-annoying ways and comparing him with this dark tempestuous, terrible character, wondering why the latter is so fascinating," she confessed to Henrietta.

They were riding in a snowstorm when he finally declared himself. "It's killing me." She was so terrified, she could barely speak. He shouted,

"If you won't speak to me, I will not see you again." It was a promise he couldn't keep even after she wrote him a letter, terminating their friendship. During their next encounter he held his tongue, and that was enough to justify seeing him again. She had reconciled herself to the facts. "He is a man whom any woman might love but whom no sane woman would marry."

Isabella knew where to draw the line with dangerous men. Do I? The rules that governed her sense of propriety and behavior no longer apply.

December 10, 1873: It was sunny but arctic cold when Jim rode with Isabella to Longmont. That night, they sat in the kitchen of the inn, warming themselves by the stove as he recited some of his poetry.

Once again she implored him to give up his whiskey. "I despise a man of your intellect being a slave to such a vice." His position remained unchanged. It was too late. As he had told her before, "It binds me hand and foot; I cannot give up the only pleasure I have." He prayed that God would give him a good death. Next morning, he stood beside his white mare and watched as Isabella boarded the coach. It wasn't until after it had pulled out of the village that she allowed herself to look out the window. Jim was leading his horse across the snowy plains, back to Estes Park. He looked like the man Isabella imagined him to be in his youth, his curly gray hair bleached blond in the sunlight. When the stagecoach pulled into Greeley, she looked back one more time. "The Rocky Mountains, and all that they enclose," had sunk below the prairie sea.

9

Vanishing Act

San Juan Range, summer solstice, 1979: My turn to tie into the umbilical cord, the dangling rope. I start around the corner, and the route to the top of Dallas Peak disappears into thin air, like Karl did forty-five minutes ago when he took the lead. Once my eyes adjust to the glare, I realize I'm standing on a snowed-in ledge that leans away from the mountain, toward Blue Lake two thousand feet below. My postholes in the snow can't take the heat at this altitude, and the only sane route back to terra firma collapses.

The ledge looks like it will run out soon and then what? Dump me? I break the golden rule and look down into the bottomless void and pray for a search and rescue chopper. Maybe I can fake a sprained ankle. Except for an occasional tug on the rope and his disembodied "Off rope!" Karl hasn't kept in touch. I shout at him to tighten the rope. The wind thunders. He can't possibly hear me. The rope jerks to maximum tension. He must be up there somewhere, guiding the rope, protecting us both with properly placed chocks and slings. If I slip and his anchor fails, the rope in his lap might unwind in a heartbeat, seizing him by the ankles, and we'll both fall.

A bonk rattles my helmet, then another. The rocks have found their bull's-eye: the black X that I taped to the top of my helmet for good luck. I shake off the debris. Three chocks nest on the buckle to my climbing harness. Karl's protection must have popped loose and slid down the rope. "Tighten!" I yell. The wind howls back. The rope doesn't move. My shouts will never reach him.

At the end of the ledge looms a thank-God-there-is-a-chimney of consolation to mountaineers with vertigo like me. The chimney is filled with rotten snow and flying shrapnel. Either I commit to the climb or shriek at Karl to feed me more rope for the retreat.

I flail at the first move until the front points of my crampons catch. Left point, right point, ice axe swinging at any mark in the rock that resembles a crack. An unorthodox technique to be sure, but I don't give a damn. I've reached the summit. I crawl past my reflection in the eye of Karl's fifty-five millimeter lens and sit as far from the edge as possible.

Will wraps his arm around my shoulders for the summit self-portrait. I manage a victory smile. Of the one hundred highest peaks in Colorado, we have just climbed the toughest one. Eighty-six down. Fourteen to go. Karl researches the access and the routes; I keep score with checkmarks and dates in the margins of our list.

In the required Colorado Mountain Club course for aspiring trip leaders, the instructor drills us in the art of tying knots, handling the rope, and rappelling. The double figure eight is the most difficult knot for me to learn and remember. I have to withdraw enough rope from the coil to loop it twice into a figure eight. In such a tight embrace, the parallel knots are practically indistinguishable. It takes a half-dozen tries to trace the second loop around the first one without kinking the rope. I have to trace the pattern of the first loop exactly.

My double figure eight achieved, I check both locks on my carabiner gate twice, as instructed, then walk backward toward the edge, clutching the dangling end of the rope in my right hand.

"Let the rope glide through your left hand as you back off the edge and lean away from the rock," the instructor says. "Your feet will balance you."

I stand on the edge of the cliff, my eyes on the hand that is supposed to control the rate of descent, and not the bottom of the cliff, another instruction.

"Don't rush or clutch the rope. It will burn. Take your time, lean back, and trust your feet."

I look at him for reassurance. He grins and gives me a thumbs-up. "If you hug the rock, you might get tangled up in the rope, and we'll have a hell of a time extricating you."

On the rappel off the summit of Dallas Peak, I get carried away with excitement and go too fast and lean too far back. My feet lose their grip, and I turn upside down and hang by my harness, twisting in the breeze.

"Grab the rope," Karl hollers down when he finally hears my shrieks. "Pull yourself back up with the rope."

At first I do not believe him. The rope will break, or I will yank him off with me.

"Take hold of the rope and pull yourself upright. I've got you." The rope judders. He is reeling in the slack so I won't bounce and strain the rope with more weight than it can support.

I reach up and grab hold. The rope swivels and sways. My head and torso right themselves, a stunned hummingbird restored to flight, fluttering toward salvation. Karl's chocks and slings, and my double figure eight, hold.

Sierras, August 1980: The granite spires of Mount Whitney's east face soar above our campsite below Iceberg Lake, making a mockery of the exposure and elevation gains to which we're accustomed in the Colorado Rockies. We're on Karl's turf now. "We won't be climbing any of the fifth-class routes," he declares. We won't be doing the tourist route on the south side either. Mobbed by hikers and runners every day of the week, it hardly qualifies as a pristine mountaineering experience. Not many of those left in his native Sierras, Karl grouses.

To reach the summit from the northeast, we have to ascend a gully to a notch and from there a steep snowfield. The climb begins at Iceberg Lake. I spot a shortcut to the lake after we depart from our campsite, and take off. When Karl finally catches up, he shouts, "I told you to stop. When I tell you to stop, I mean stop. We're not going to separate."

What a hypocrite. He's always leaving me behind. If he had followed me this time, we could have shaved an hour off a twelve-hour day. My route was more direct.

"A is for asshole. B is for bastard. C is for . . . ," I mutter under my breath.

"What did you say?"

I swallow my rage and let him take the lead, even though I frequently have to wait as he winds his way through the boulders. When we reach the upper snowfield, the climb proves more treacherous than we anticipated. The surface refroze in the night, forming a crust that splinters with each kick step. One misstep and we won't stop sliding for two thousand feet. Karl is carrying a rope but no ice screws. We left our ice axes and crampons at home. With his bigger boots, Karl stomps in a plank of steps that gives me more confidence than my shallower kick steps. I implore him to stay close so I can stop calculating the probability of a fall and focus on the next toehold.

The summit ridge is free of snow, and Karl makes good time until the last few steps. He pauses, a look of wonder on his face. The head and feet of a man poke out of an upright redwood box with both ends sawed off. Maybe this is some magician's trick. We're not that far from Hollywood.

"An open-air latrine," Karl surmises. "At least you can see the view from there." A Boy Scout troop is lined up at the door, waiting for their leader to finish his business so they can each take their turn.

We clear the only unoccupied rock on the summit of its running sneakers, pink fanny pack, and half-eaten turkey, sun-dried tomato, and Teleme cheese sandwich so we can admire the smog. "Positively nuclear," Karl says, munching on his stale gorp.

Elk Range, October 11, 1981: The tourists have gone home, defeated by the cold, resigned to the resumption of habitual routine. We are the only party on the mountain. Somewhere above us, lost in mist, the last mountain on our centennial-peaks list awaits us. It has no name.

We exit the stand of Engelmann and blue spruce where we pitched our tent and pass Conundrum Hot Springs, bathing ourselves in the drifting steam. Braced for the ascent, we advance on the tipping saucer of the rock-strewn tundra. Patches of skunk cabbage sag in rusted heaps, smelling of moldy library books. The higher we hike, the dicier the weather. Clouds swirl around us like smoke from a rampaging wildfire. Graupel assails us from nearly every direction, stinging our cheeks with first-degree burns. Karl consults his compass so we can navigate in the fog and shouts directions at me so he can be heard above the cacophony of the wind. The wind pastes icicles onto his beard, sucks us dry, bends us into withered, old hunchbacks.

We totter on, driven by our determination to complete a nearly decade-long project. The celebration on the summit is brief. Karl wears his wedding tuxedo, clutching the top hat he purchased at Salvation Army with one hand so it won't blow off in the wind. His fluttering tie and the ruffled hem of the turquoise nightgown I wear over my climbing attire intertwine like the necks of courting swans. We name our nameless peak Mount Gray because of the similarity between the rock and the weather, and the contrast with our mood.

Mission accomplished. I am the first woman to climb the one hundred highest peaks of Colorado.

Our celebration resumes in the hot springs among friends who have backpacked in a bottle of champagne and a floating tray of gourmet delicacies for the occasion. Deviled curried eggs, cranberry goat cheese and Breton crackers, homemade angel food cake dipped in melted Ghirardelli chocolate. Having skipped the summit bid in favor of a prolonged soak, they withhold their congratulatory greetings until we strip and climb in. Then the cork pops and the foam spurts. We lift our champagne glasses for the toast.

The dreaded storm never materializes fully, more bluster than substance, as was the case during the ascent. In our microclimate of comingled steam and breath, we lose track of time, the onset of night. In the shrouded moonlight, our albino cheeks and iced eyelashes substitute for absent stars. I wish I had Karl all to myself.

At midnight our friends fish us out, wrinkled and helpless as newborn twins. Disentangling our entwined limbs, they dress me first, not entirely in my own clothes. It takes two men to prop up Karl. Our escorts hang on to us all the way back to camp so we don't tip over or squash the tent. The zipper magically opens; our sleeping bags are readied for reentry. Hauling me by the neck, they tuck me in before shoving Karl in beside me. He falls asleep the moment his head rolls into his sleeping-bag hood, his cheeks still toasty from our lengthy soak.

Soon I nod off only to be jostled awake by Karl's snoring and the flapping of our slack tent fly in the blustery breeze. I crawl out of my bag, unzip the fly, stick my head out. The storm has blown through, depositing plump cushions of snow on the bushes and tree stumps where we sorted our gear yesterday morning. The aspen limbs are whiskered in white. Evergreen boughs droop from the plenitude of the storm's hit-and-run Epiphany offering. I risk the cold, fortifying myself with Karl's down jacket.

On my return from our designated latrine, I flop on my back, carving angels out of a freezing mattress. The moon has broken through, inescapable and inexhaustible. The sight of it transports me back to the dawn of an ice age and the formation of a mountain range. The mountains still stand as time reverses and races into the future. Empires rise and fall; new species are birthed in the wake of mass extinctions. A familiar flower survives. Lady's slippers dangle their pink lips over the shaded soil where my ashes were scattered eons ago, paying homage to the Greek goddess of love. A blast of wind on chilled skin brings my imagined journey to a halt. I crawl back in beside Karl, my fingers too numb to work the zippers that will release us from our separate pods. I place my hands inside my undershirt, against my heart, in hopes of a revival by dawn.

At daybreak, I roll over and extend my arm to give Karl a hug. His sleeping bag is occupied by someone else. It takes me a while to remember what really happened. He left long before nightfall, rushing back to our campsite as I lingered in the hot springs with our drunken friends. He had to pack out in time to prepare for a Monday morning meeting. One of our companions took his place, too unsteady on his feet to make it to his own tent.

My copy of the celebratory summit photo sits on my desk, fading beneath the dust, until I decide to give it to my mother for Christmas. The last time I saw it in Kansas City, I realized I had gotten some of those details wrong, too. My windblown nightgown balloons at the stomach, a size more suitable for maternity leave than mountaineering. If I really had been pregnant, Karl would have had something to celebrate besides the completion of our centennial-peak list.

He tried to impregnate me once atop another unnamed peak. Afterward he named it Conception Peak even though the union failed to conceive. He kept his disappointment to himself. Babies were one of those subjects to be avoided at all costs. We talked about the unclimbed mountains on our list, about equipment and Colorado politics and the depressing state of world affairs and the environment (especially when the Republicans were in charge of the White House), but we rarely talked about our relationship, especially in bed. Or Karl's desire to have children and my reluctance for fear we were too ill equipped. Both topics off limits, a violation of a tacit agreement.

10

Slippery

Karl is on the road again, installing spook software for the military—code-scramblers to confuse the enemy. Highly classified material. Disclosing the exact nature of his business would jeopardize his security clearance. He flies to Boston and Las Vegas and Sydney, Australia. One night I track him down by phone at the Hyatt in Philadelphia. He doesn't have time to talk, he says. It must be a poor connection because I have to ask him to repeat himself. Static on the line, or is that a clink of glass in the background, a playful smacking of lips? They can't be his lips. His lips are occupied with the phone.

"You have a visitor?" I visualize a blonde of Norwegian ancestry. On the beaches of his native Los Angeles, most of the women look Scandinavian.

"It's practically midnight," he says. "Why are you calling at this hour?"

"Who is in your room?"

"No one is in my room. I have a single. I always do. You know this."

Is the purpose of every trip top secret? I've wondered before. His behavior at home has raised questions. His overly generous tips to waitresses, canceled dates, all those late nights at work. But my lips are sealed. Karl believed me when no one else did. And I have a family history, which makes my mind suspect.

As a child I thought nothing of my father's muttered conversations with imaginary, seemingly more attentive companions than us. With three females in the household, he often retreated to the only space he claimed as his own—his mind. The monologue addressed to the dining room table as supper was served signaled his return to the family fold.

But after Alice's commitment to the state hospital at age twenty-one, Dad's eccentricities intruded on the future I imagined for myself—my fate possibly foretold as well as hers.

Two-and-a-half years after her initial diagnosis at Menninger's, my parents consulted a specialist in schizophrenia. Psychoanalysis every week, daily doses of Thorazine, shock therapy as a last resort—her suffering persisted, the downhill course of her disease unaltered. The doctor leveled with my mother, who was determined to care for Alice at home, to keep spinning for the right combination that would set her free. The doctor told her what no other doctor was willing to admit: "She has the most severe form of schizophrenia there is. It's not your fault; it's no one's fault. There is no cure for her illness. She needs to be hospitalized not only for her sake but for the sake of your marriage."

During my annual trips to Kansas City, I visit Alice at the state hospital. She sits on the orange vinyl sofa in her ward, in her stained dress and torn stockings, monitored and supervised so she doesn't snatch a cup of coffee from another patient or grab the phone and place a collect call to Olympian Jim Ryun or the White House. The highlight of her day, the lineup before each meal, hands outstretched for the dispensation of meds. Monday and Wednesday afternoon swim, Friday morning workshop assembling fish lures for Goodwill Industries. She sits there, with unshaved, parted legs, making baby talk to Twiggy, her beloved doll reduced to rags after ten years in the state hospital. Half a dozen antipsychotic drug regimens over the years have kept the voices at bay, the outbursts in check, but her twitching feet never rest, and her tongue darts in and out of corkscrewed lips. The trade-offs for subduing the worst symptoms of a little-understood illness once attributed to demonic possession and witchcraft.

Perhaps Karl is worried about my family history, too, and that's why he pays so much attention to my wardrobe. When I wear used clothes from the Salvation Army (a size too large for better concealment), he calls me the Bag Lady. I hope the gauzy, floor-length gown I purchased at Filthy Wilma's, the vintage clothing and jewelry shop at the mouth of Ruxton Canyon, will be more to his liking. It is made of cotton, not satin, but that isn't the problem. The puffed sleeves, dainty violets, and off-white lace are too childish for his taste, though he doesn't mind the plunging neckline beneath the lace. Perhaps the dress reminds him of the age difference. "Are you Daddy's girl?" he asks on more than one occasion. I hope he's joking.

I feel courageous when I wear the dress, even though the lace barely conceals the cavity in my chest from my birth defect. I host tea parties for my lady friends, a more sympathetic, approving audience, especially when lubricated with a shot of brandy in each cup. That's as far as I dare go. The showgirls on the Moulin Rouge poster I hung above the sofa dance for me with their kicking legs and raised skirts. Karl is unable to attend. He is too busy earning a living for both of us.

However I calculate my worth—in dollars and cents or the size of our footprints in the world—his job, helping to defend the homeland from a Soviet missile strike—outweighs mine on both accounts. My part-time magazine internship provides a steadier source of income than substitute teaching. Enough income to buy all the groceries and sock away some savings. Rather than carrying out someone else's lesson plans, I'm stepping out into the world to report on contentious city council meetings, downtown revitalization projects, and lesser-known hiking destinations well worth the effort. In comparison to Isabella Bird's sure-footed prose, my stories wander aimlessly, novice that I am, in search of an organizing principle, or they labor under the excessive influence of successful outdoor adventure writers, all men, whose exploits in the backcountry put mine to shame. Sometimes I sit in front of the computer waiting for the words to magically appear. It doesn't occur to me that I have a perspective to offer. If I go deep, I might trespass on private property or disappear like my father, gone for good.

How else does one learn except by trial and error? For all my doubt, I produce more content than anyone else on the staff without blowing a single deadline. The desire to enlarge my footprint overcomes my lack of confidence. But when it comes to the physical sensations I disowned after the rape, I look outward for expression. Filthy Wilma's heavily made-up face on the brick exterior of my favorite shop is the mask I don to conceal my real face. Even in paint on such a hard surface, her face offers a container into which I can pour my sexual desire. Wilma's face becomes my face with the makeup I buy at J.C. Penney's at a price I can afford.

With a shock I notice the resemblance to Alice at sixteen, disembarking from her flight from Los Angeles in a sleeveless, tropical-fruited orange silk shift, floppy white raffia hat, and big bronze sunglasses, a long bamboo cigarette holder pinched between her fingers, her eyelashes overly thickened with too many coats of black mascara. Alice had brown eyelashes. She did not smoke. She eschewed colors that singled her out. In 1965 a virtuous young woman did not paint her face like a whore's.

I think too much. That's why I stay up half the night. If I were one of Ida's girls, I could take the cure at the spa. Instead, I follow the advice of the billboard campaign that directs the tourists off Highway 24, into the overwrought heart of Manitou's downtown shopping district. Between the July 4th fireworks display that sets the steep mountainside behind Ruxton House ablaze and the Labor Day weekend festivities that cushion the blow of yet another school year, I often sit at the bottom of our staircase, watching the Greyhound buses cruise up the avenue en route to the Pikes Peak Cog Railway. They come and go, the passengers' views of the overbuilt hillsides obscured by tinted windows and lowered sun visors. Or I stroll down the avenue, past Filthy Wilma's and Muzzleloaders Outfitters, and turn right for a genuine kitsch window-shopping experience on Manitou Boulevard. Ignoring the displays of made-in-Taiwan moccasins and imitation turquoise rings, I bypass the loiterers outside the Ancient Mariner Tavern and sit on the closest bench to Patsy's red-and-white-striped gazebo. A line of tourists stretches from the window halfway down the block. The scent of butterscotch and cheddar cheese popcorn and of lemon and peppermint salt-water taffy has lured them out of their air-conditioned El Dorados. They do not realize their children have been spirited away until they lick the salt from their lips and hear the gunfire, whistles, and shrieks coming from the Penny Arcade across the footbridge, on the other side of the creek.

I haven't realized it yet, but I am a tourist, too, just passing through, unable to resist temptation, a sucker for false advertising and hype. On the return trip I compare the sales pitches at the Irish linen shops: "All merchandise 75% off!" at Shamrock's; "Going Out of Business! Prices, a Steal!" at his competitor's across the street. The same claims they've been making for years. I'm beginning to suspect that marriage is also a business transaction, seller and buyer bargaining for the best terms. As long as the defects are disclosed and covered by the warranty, the transaction should satisfy both.

Karl has no time for sightseeing or speculating. He has more important responsibilities on his mind. Walls must be knocked down, a kitchen modernized, a walkway and deck rebuilt before they give up the ghost. He tackles the living and dining rooms first. The wall in between, a Depression-era addition, must go to make room for the dining room table. He sets up his table saw in the kitchen—what's left of it in the aftermath of a well-intentioned, incomplete plumbing relocation project, and goes to work in a cloud of construction dust, shredded cobwebs, and shattered plaster. Despite the occasional curse, he seems as content with his work as our recently adopted cat with the mice she stalks from her hiding place in an unfinished cabinet. Karl has found his mission in life: the restoration of the historic and structural integrity of the house.

I oversee the fruit orchard and garden. The peaches have been chewed to their pits, their branches partially defoliated. Karl strings more strands of barbed wire to the fence, and the mule deer sail over to finish their feast. A prolonged heat wave has not only decimated their preferred forage but subjected the vegetable garden to a grasshopper invasion. They hop up and down, clicking their castanets in rhythm with their diabolic Mexican hat dance. Nothing is spared. The Bibb lettuce, zucchini, and sugar peas mowed into matchsticks. A month's planting laid waste in a matter of days. The bent cornstalks remain standing despite the miscarriage of their de-kerneled husks. I could have fought back with malathion but that would have defeated the purpose of chemical-free gardening.

There will be no canned vegetables or fruit preserves in the pantry to sustain us over the winter. My primary contribution (besides vacuuming) to the containment of the household budget must await a more propitious planting.

July seemed so promising. The thunderclouds would build over Pikes Peak by early afternoon, as they often did this time of year, and a rain shower would follow, settling the dust, alleviating the heat.

On July 31, 1976, our second summer at Ruxton House, a thunderstorm rolls in later than usual. It is the eve of the state centennial, and an unrehearsed fireworks display of lightning, punctuated by booms that ricochet across the canyon, preempts the public celebration.

The timing isn't the only noteworthy aspect of the storm. Rather than a short-lived cloudburst that clears out as suddenly as it starts, this thunderstorm is unlike any on record—a stationary downpour that rattles and films over windows, chills the whole house. We huddle beside the radio, listening to the weather updates. Suddenly a groan outside, then a thud that shakes the cracked foundation of the house. The house doesn't budge. We rush outside, into the sobbing dementia of the storm. The earth slid. The slope behind the house with no retaining wall has shed its Great Basin wild rye and Rocky Mountain thistle. The staircase we ascend every morning to the upper lot bursts into a waterfall of mud and debris. If we don't hold back the earth, it will bury our house. Karl grabs a shovel and starts digging a dam of uprooted bushes, grass, and gravel. I run back inside and turn up the radio. Flash flood in Big Thompson Canyon. Nearly a year's worth of rain has fallen in several hours, and a tower of water twenty feet high is roaring down the river gorge below Estes Park, one hundred miles to the north, taking out everything in its path: cottonwoods, cabins, propane tanks, pickups. Into the roiling carnage is swept a thirty-ton water pipe, ripped out of its concrete moorings, and an unknown number of campers and residents who fail to make high ground or hear the warnings in time.

I rush back outside and rejoin Karl. We shovel despite the burning in our chests, shaking off the droplets like dunked dogs. No matter what obstacle we throw in its path, the migrating earth gains ground on the back of the house. Karl works through the night, hauling and slinging sandbags to reinforce the remaining slope. I help until my lower back freezes up. My body is spent.

I wonder how George Ruxton felt, helpless before the fire that chased him off the mountainside in the middle of the night. An Arapaho hunting party had spotted his pack mules. The fire they set ignited in the parched timber and brush; fanned by a brisk breeze, the flames spread almost as fast as Ruxton and his mules could run. When he reached the Arkansas River, seven miles away, he watched the enlarging and merging torches that lit the night sky and illuminated Pikes Peak as if it were high noon. His venison stew and jerky had been left behind, his rifle was soaked from the panic-stricken creek crossing, and the nearest fort was more than a day's march, but he had escaped with his scalp still attached.

Karl turns back the flood in time to save the house. Next morning, we survey the damage. The foundation and front yard are still intact, and Ruxton House is in no danger of collapsing or sliding off the cliff. A vigorous hosing will take care of the mess out back. The toll from the Big Thompson Canyon flood will take months to calculate: two million dollars in property damage, one hundred forty-three dead.

The renovation of the interior requires patience, tenacity, attention to detail. Sometimes the project is completed to Karl's satisfaction; more often than not, he abandons it to start another. His mission in life fulfills him, this husband of mine, wielding a crowbar and clawhammer. Room by room he strips the walls to the studs, exposing a maze of rusted lead pipes, frayed copper wiring, and decaying newspaper insulation. Advertisements from the November 8, 1911, edition of the *Pikes Peak Journal* float through the air—miniature B. F. Goodrich hot-air balloons proclaiming the benefits of Tutt's Insomnia Pills and Carmichael's

Honey and Tar Cough Suppressant and Dr. Sainsbury's treatments for dyspeptic ladies.

Saturday afternoons Karl emerges from the rubble to shop the antique auctions for bargains: a marble-topped end table, a china cabinet with curved glass and claw feet, a mirrored credenza with sliding, beveled glass door. He hauls a trailer full of family heirlooms from his mother's house in Los Angeles and shields them in white sheets from the construction dust.

For the Halloween party at the haunted Ruxton House, I string fake cobwebs over the sheets and arrange our bed pillows into the body of a corpse. The head consists of a pillowcase stuffed with Karl's soiled shirts. Dozens of friends from the Colorado Mountain Club show up, some from as far away as Denver. They carry ropes in their knapsacks, as the invitation recommended, for the climb in the dark up the seventy-two steps. My portrayal of Alice's Queen of Hearts is so convincing, every animal in the house except the dog runs for its life. Karl tracks them down in his undertaker's costume and opens the closet door. When Mighty Mouse and Tony the Tiger and the White Rabbit try to escape, I swing my croquet mallet and shout, "Off with their heads!"

The walls—what's left of them—have come alive with the scratching of claws and scampering of feet. Someday I will recall these events, a dozen years after we moved into Ruxton House, with amusement, but not now, not in the middle of the night. I grope for the covers and pull them to my neck. The dog is curled up on the edge of the mattress, fast asleep and oblivious to the pair of red embers glowing at us in the darkness. I reach for the bedside lamp, but before I can throw it a flicking white tail reveals the identity of the intruder. The dog sits up and growls without giving chase—chastened by the previous intruder, a raccoon that entered through the cat window in the kitchen. Of its own accord the wood rat scurries back to its warren for the winter, disappearing into the same maze where his mate and their growing brood have been hunting for food and nesting material. With so many holes to choose from, they circulate with ease, tunneling deeper and deeper into the bowels of the house, propagating their species.

Karl's sledgehammer has been ruthlessly efficient. It has knocked so many holes in the walls, the partition between me and the past crumbles. I am a teenager again in Kansas City, Alice still living at home. Three men in black uniforms, nightsticks drawn, motion to my father to accompany them. Then they return for my sister, who has accused our father of rape. Shrieked her accusation at the top of her lungs so that the filthy, unspeakable, damning words exit the stadium and cross the state line, penetrating the fundamentalist hinterlands of Kansas and Missouri. "Get your fucking fingers out of my throat!" I sit beside their vacant seats as Len Dawson's pass to Mike Garrett connects and Garrett hurtles into the end zone. The umpire flashes a V with raised arms, and the crowd leaps to its feet, submerging my sobs with their cheers. Dad didn't lay a finger on her. I sat next to them until the police came. The stadium is nearly empty when they return. Alice's psychiatrist confirmed the veracity of Dad's statement. She was hallucinating.

I may be hallucinating myself. It is five thirty in the morning, the exact moment the soldier who raped me crawled onto my bed. The mattress I am lying on now is facing the wrong direction. The needle of my internal compass, my head and feet, is lined up on the east-to-west axis. I must be sleeping in an unfamiliar place, a motel room perhaps. Where is Karl? The dog? His muddy paw prints stain the window glass. He must have tired of waiting for me to let him back in. The drip from the sink faucet in the adjacent bathroom locates me in the sitting room. The master bedroom is out of commission, a thinly veiled statement perhaps about the condition of our conjugal relationship. Karl gutted the room before leaving for Utah on another top-secret mission.

Alice could not be believed. Her mind had snapped. The psychiatrist said as much. I was perfectly sane when I called the police. Here are the underpants he removed. This is the knife he put to my throat. There must be fingerprints. Think I'm making this up? Look at the jimmied

window in my spare bedroom. Still don't believe me? My hand holds
the knife. When I lift the blade out of Karl's razor, it nicks my thumb.
Unsatisfactory. Not one drop of blood. I press the tip of one edge into
my right forearm. The same arm I painted blue in retaliation for Martha
Gunther's false accusation in Miss Lund's third-grade art class. I did not
spill the paint. Martha did. I'm innocent not only of that charge but all
the other charges spinning through my mind. I'm not a locked safe to
be picked, a specimen on a stainless-steel table, a hopeless psychotic like
my sister. Not a child in adult clothing vying for her Sugar Daddy's love
and protection. Or so I try to convince myself for fear of being unworthy
of Karl's love. His love my only sanctuary in a capricious world.

Three pricks, with the attentive detachment of a nurse taking samples.
A slash would be too messy and risky, thwarting the point of the exercise.
I don't want to kill myself. I want to see blood.

The blood poured out of Rocky Mountain Jim as he lay on the ground,
his horse shot dead beside him, his pistol undrawn. Three of the bullets
had passed right through him, as if he were indestructible. The fourth
bullet shattered his nose. They took him to the hospital in Fort Collins
and the speed of his recovery astonished the doctors. Soon he was well
enough to be seen on the streets, so it was a surprise when he suddenly
took a turn for the worse and lapsed into a coma. Rocky Mountain Jim
was shot in June 1874. He died in September, as the cottonwoods and
withered clematis and Virginia creeper alongside the North St. Vrain
were turning gold and crimson, just as Isabella described it the year
before during her first ride up the canyon en route to Estes Park.

The coroner found two fragments in the back of Jim's brain. This was
the fifth bullet. It had fractured his skull. Griff Evans was arrested but never
tried. He said Jim was drunk and vile and threatening, and he shot him in
self-defense. Before he died, Jim said Griff shot him because of his refusal
to sell out. Griff had sold his ranch to Lord Dunraven and Jim was the
only holdout. Some people said Jim flirted too much with Griff's daughter.

Isabella heard five different versions of his death. But by then she had distanced herself. "Don't let anybody think that I was in love with Rocky Mountain Jim," she wrote a friend. "It was pity and yearning to save him that I felt."

Isabella's romance with Rocky Mountain Jim flickered to life in her imagination and there it stayed, her public persona untainted, beyond reproach. The publication of *A Lady's Life in the Rocky Mountains* would launch her career as one of the most popular travel writers of her time. More books and articles would follow, recounting her impressions of Japan, Malaya, Persia, Tibet, Korea, and China. She was the first woman to be appointed a fellow of the Royal Geographic Society. Traditionalists objected, one of whom contested "the general ability of women to contribute to scientific geographical knowledge. Their sex and training render them equally unfitted for exploration."

My imagination has strayed even farther off the beaten path, into fictional territory. And I don't even know it.

11

Free Fall

My therapist calls it a five-week date rape. I call it something else. Grounds for divorce? I didn't solicit, but I didn't protest either. After thirteen years of marriage, I've finally called it quits without admitting it.

I am thirty-eight and restless. He is a friend of a friend. Eyes the color of glacial meltwater. Canyon explorer and collector of Southwest Indian art. His documentaries of the genocidal drug wars in Latin America nearly costing him his life more than once. The suicide of his estranged son prophesized by a masked dancer at Shalako, the Zuni winter solstice ceremony. Shaking his rattler at him, he spoke in perfect English. "He will shoot himself in the mouth."

I offer my guest a glass of wine. He is careful not to spill it on my burgundy velvet sofa. He takes a sip and tells me another story, stranger than the suicide prediction. He was driving across the reservation one misty night when he saw an old woman walking alongside the road. A shapeless figure wearing a scarf, leaning on a stick. He braked, thinking she was a hitchhiker. Instead of a face, he saw the eyes and beak of an owl. When he looked into his rearview mirror, she was gone, a phantom of the mist or a skinwalker. "Navajo witchcraft," he explains. An ordinary human by day, an evildoer in animal form at night, a skinwalker must slay a loved one to procure its power.

He invites me on a camping trip in November, a hell of a time to hike in the desert. I consult Karl. "I don't have to go. Would you rather I didn't?"

"Go. I have to work over the holidays." A statement he will regret. Just one word. A kiss. And I would have changed my mind. But his back is turned and he is kneeling, adjusting the valve on the radiator. Doesn't he give a damn? Or maybe he cares more about the house.

Pulled hard, the cords of memory snarl and knot, disrupting the chronological narrative, rendering it incoherent. I can reconstruct bits and pieces of the journey and topography, but not the act other than its tireless redundancy. His advances and her acquiescence easier to justify in the isolation of their first campsite, beneath the turquoise ring of cloud that wrapped itself around the moon, constricting it. The sand dunes at their back, white as death. The black hulk of the Sangre de Cristos hunched over the silver serpent of the river. The sin of their adultery washed away in the sand. Except there is a witness. The fawn that lifts its head from its mother's nipple.

Next morning, they drive away before the rest of the campers get up. She looks back once; the sand has covered their tracks—her last glimpse of Colorado. She relinquishes her car keys. She relinquishes everything: her willpower, her self-respect and dignity. He does all the driving, most of the talking. She doesn't say much because her mind has drifted off to some dreamscape that seems more tangible than the fractured landscape on the horizon. She wishes he would slow down. He's taking her beyond the blue mountains into renegade Indian country, where the earth is skinned to the bone, its back broken, and lonesome mesas and petrified sand dunes rise up and float away like apparitions. He's following the escape route of Butch Cassidy and the Sundance Kid and losing the posse in the slickrock of southern Utah, the coyote trickster of his laughter bouncing off the canyon walls to further confuse the lawmen.

Thanksgiving with the turkey vultures in Sheiks Canyon. They have to ford the icy creek in their bare feet to reach the pictographs of horned serpents and headless torsos painted in blood and urine, Kokopelli, the flute player, mocking them with his monstrosity of a penis. Inflating the size of his, which can't have enough of her. In the tent, on the trail, in an alcove beneath the masked deities of a migratory people.

The fiftieth anniversary of Pearl Harbor on a dirt road to nowhere, the trail lost, the tent pitched in the dark, in the deepest, remotest canyon of them all. Separated from friends and family, home and work. Her bloody underpants impossible to cleanse in the dried-up wash. Her pain the source of his pleasure.

They cross the treeless, wind-scoured border into New Mexico, the sand stinging her eyes through the shut vents.

Winter solstice among the ruins of a ceremonial center. High up Fajada Butte the sun will drive its daggers into the shafts where the high priests pecked their spiral calendars. A sight her captor and she will never see. The rangers have closed the trail to protect a vulnerable heritage. And she's trapped in the tent. Like the Puebloans whose rituals and warfare grew more extreme in the face of drought, spent resources, and malnutrition, he's a desperate man resorting to desperate measures.

Christmas Eve in a Pueblo chapel, the priest praying for their souls in English, Spanish, and Tanoan, as if redemption were still possible in any language.

New Year's Eve in a neon-lit motel, a wooden Indian outside, the grunts of fatigue and showers next door and canned laughter accompanying Johnny Carson's monologue a welcome muffler to her feigned moans. He watches her constantly, his eyes more like the burnt coals of a Charles Manson or a Ted Bundy than an alpine lake. Why didn't she notice until now? The fireworks go off at midnight; he shows no signs of wearing out. He's been popping Percodans the whole trip. The bottle is in the pocket of his shed hiking pants. When he isn't looking, she reaches in and shakes it. It must be half empty. An uncorked champagne bottle sits on the nightstand. She pours her portion into the bathroom sink, flushing the toilet simultaneously to conceal the deed. At the rate he's drinking, the combination of alcohol and narcotics will knock him out, and she can steal away into the night in her coyote skin, her medicine more potent than his. But he keeps waking up and rolling over to cop another round.

"You alright, hon?" the proprietor's wife asks when they drop the key off at the front desk in the morning. She can't be trusted to do it by herself.

He suspects, correctly, that she will cut and run unless every bridge is burned. He has the bigger vocabulary, the superior intellect, so she lets him dictate the terms. She wishes she could blame her compliance on sorcery, but that would be a lie. Her fingers steered the pen, her tongue licked the envelopes. One letter for her parents, another for Karl. He drops them into the slot so she doesn't pull a fast one.

The significance of the Pearl Harbor date eludes her until the first interview with the psychiatrist on her return to civilization. December 7th, the anniversary of the rape, the day her free will was torpedoed and sunk to the bottom of the ocean.

Karl gives her a second chance. Even her therapist can testify she was out of her mind and her lover a psychopath. She's got the pill bottles to prove it. Trilafon, a modest dose; she's not as sick as her schizophrenic sister. "You'll notice the difference in five to six weeks," her therapist assures her. Lorazepam for the anxiety that makes her skin crawl and her feet twitch. Ambien for sleeping, which does the job for a while. A week in a psychiatric hospital with a heroin-addicted prostitute for a roommate and a Vietnam vet down the hall who boasts of the penises he cut off his Vietcong prisoners. In art therapy she draws a picture of a warped head with a penis in its mouth. She doesn't say much during group therapy. Her story seems so inconsequential in comparison to the musician who was raped repeatedly by her father. She agrees to biweekly counseling. She wants out. And now that she has emerged from the shadows, she can acknowledge she needs help. She can't fix her messed-up mind by herself.

Can her therapist write her a prescription for staying awake? Karl has taken her back but she wonders how long that will last. He married a skinwalker—half human, half beast.

Her feminine intuition is still intact. Karl has to work late. His boss is afraid of their new boss. The company has sold, rumors of pink slips for Christmas circulate among middle-aged employees, and Karl will soon turn fifty. He doesn't show up for the outdoor concert at Memorial Park. At the last minute he cancels their dinner date at their favorite French restaurant. If there is a weekend hike on the agenda, a sure bet, she can no longer count on him because he frequently breaks that date, too. The dog does his best to keep up with her in the mountains, but his hips are wearing out.

"Are you in love with Louise?" she asks him in counseling. She would have asked him sooner, but she dismissed her suspicions as the delusional thinking of a deranged woman.

"No, of course not. Don't be absurd."

"You're spending an awful lot of time with her so I can't help but wonder."

"Well, you've got it wrong."

She digs at the dirt in her nails from the previous weekend's hike with the dog. "I believe you, I do."

Karl digs the pit on the only level, foliage-free site near the house—the spot where the earth slid and nearly washed away the foundation. Unless the cloud cover blots it out, the blinding fireball of the sun will rise here every morning, lighting the city below before reaching their sanctuary.

Karl wraps the dog in his blue blanket and lowers him into the pit. It is raining hard. She doesn't know why her face is so wet. The rain? Tears? The casting of dirt is unnecessary. Clumps of mud migrate into the pit, staining the blanket.

She put the dog to sleep before the divorce was finalized. Karl didn't want to do it so she took charge. In her new life she will not have the resources to care for a crippled dog. The divorce decree arrives on July 13th, 1991, the day after their fifteenth anniversary. They stopped seeing the marriage counselor several months before. Her dinner plate had shattered the uneasy truce struck during their last session. No one was more surprised than she. At the last second she turned and aimed the plate at the sofa instead of Karl's head. It hit the window, barely missing the stained glass.

His confession took her by surprise. She was stroking the back of his neck when he said, "That's how Louise touches me."

When the divorce decree arrives, they are standing in the kitchen, sorting dishes and utensils into his and her piles. The decree comes by mail in an envelope that makes it look like a bill. Since household expenses are still primarily Karl's responsibility, he is the one who rips the envelope open. When he looks up at her, she thinks he is going to tell her that she owes him something. Instead, he says, "We're divorced." They both comment on the irony of the date as they look at each other in disbelief.

The rain is falling lightly two weeks later when she hands over her key to Ruxton House. She is abandoning her claim; this piece of property never belonged to her in the first place. She is giving her share back to the natives—the mule deer that descend from the steep forest at dusk, that ignore the no-trespassing signs and leap the barbed-wire fence.

The spring rains have been frequent this year, but not violently so, and the peach trees in the fruit orchard have benefited from this act of generosity. They have grown three feet since 1976, the year of the flood, and their branches are pregnant with so much fruit, the heaviest ones slump to the ground. The fruit they bore in 1976 were eaten by the deer. That was the year when promises were made that were later broken, and lightning streaked into the horizon like melting comets, and whole families were sucked into the crushing turbulence of a runaway river. Memorial services were held without caskets. The mud and debris had to be cleared before the river finally spit out its victims. At least two of the corpses were never recovered.

12

Off Belay

July 1990: I name my house Bijou, for the street outside my bay window. "Bijou" is French for delicate jewel. Karl bought this house, too, and had it renovated as a rental property. Once my name succeeds his on the title and I start paying the bills and redecorating, I will call this house Jane's House. This is the first house I have ever owned. Built in 1888 on a narrow lot, it insulates itself from the adjacent cottage with a nearly windowless exterior wall. Enough privacy for me. Traces of Manitou show in the tilting front porch. The wallpaper in the bedrooms upstairs is fingerprint-stained and worn along the light-switch plates, the siding pockmarked from exposure and age. For a century-old house, it has weathered the storms rather well.

The night before moving in, I dream of Ida Clothier's Bird Cage. In my dream it is no longer a house of ill repute but an actual bird cage with brass bars and a dome gilded in twined ivy. It appears to be unoccupied until the door opens and a gray chickadee hops onto the lip, inflating its chest and flapping its diffident wings. In flight, the bird morphs into a parrot with iridescent green plumage and an orange chest. I wonder if it will survive the change in habitat. Outside the cage, its vibrant coloring will attract predators.

Bijou is older than Ruxton House, with more upkeep required. The peeling paint on the front porch, frozen pipes in winter when the temperature dives into the single digits, taxes, insurance, and utility bills are my responsibility now. I don't begin to have enough furniture for all three bedrooms upstairs. Mindful of my budget, I shop for deals in the *Thrifty Nickel*. With the addition of a desk and file cabinet, I convert one of the bedrooms into a study. My portion of the topo maps fills an entire drawer. The trips will have to wait until after the open house. I announce the time and date on perfumed lavender cards with yellow daisies. I have something else to celebrate: my first full-time job with benefits, writing alumni magazine stories and PR copy for my alma mater.

March 1881: Isabella Bird announced her marriage on mourning stationery and wore widow's weeds to the ceremony, staggering to the altar "drunk with loss," "half-blinded with tears." She is marrying her sister's physician, the suitor she once rejected and whom her sister had hoped to marry. In her wedding portrait Isabella looks gaunt, as though she hasn't eaten for weeks. Her dull, unseeing expression resembles a death mask. Perhaps she is mourning not only the loss of her independence at fifty but the loss of her sister the previous June.

Henrietta, Isabella's confidante, scholarly muse, and selfless surrogate. The sister who stayed home, doing the charitable work expected of them both so Isabella, the invalid, could travel guilt free. For five weeks, she lay there, hyperthermic and unresponsive to Isabella's bedside prayers while Dr. Bishop and his nurse tried to reduce her temperature with bloodlettings, warm baths, and cold compresses. Henrietta's fever would not break. She slipped into a coma and died without regaining consciousness.

Whether by illness or genetic misfortune, the sisters we leave behind with our adventuring do not mean to injure us with their leave-taking. Only the suicidal choose the timing and method of their departure. Yet some part of us feels responsible, convinced that if we had devoted more time to them and indulged in fewer excursions, we could have influenced the outcome. Isabella's prayers would have been answered. My presence would have lessened the suffering.

Dr. John Bishop was a patient man. He had proposed once before, accepting Isabella's change of heart with benign resignation. "I'm scarcely a marrying woman," she had said. The ten-year age difference did not deter him, even though it must have shown on her well-traveled face.

He admired her curiosity and intellect, her acclaim as the author of five travel books. Although he failed to understand her incessant need to travel, he agreed to respect her desire to keep traveling and writing and publishing. They could sleep in separate bedrooms. It was her companionship that he sought.

The honeymoon was brief. Nine months later John Bishop fell ill after operating on a sailor with a skin infection. The doctor had a cut on his face, the likely conduit for the transmission. Isabella oversaw his care. She took him to the south coast of England, the French Riviera, the Swiss Alps, but neither the sea air nor the mountain air made any difference. He was given a blood transfusion, an experimental procedure, and it did nothing to reverse his deterioration. Inch by inch, he was wasting away, a bedridden, bright-eyed skeleton with translucent white hands. She tried to ease his pain with chloroform. Two days before their fifth anniversary, he died after promising Isabella, "I will be with you always."

It was easier to acknowledge the ghost of an unconsummated romance than the death of a husband she had come to love in the last year of their marriage. Within a month of the funeral, she was writing again. She was obsessed with a visitation twelve years before, and she tried to reconstruct the memory in prose so it could be investigated and validated by male scientists associated with the Society for Psychical Research.

She was lying in bed in her hotel room when she looked up and saw Rocky Mountain Jim gazing down at her. "I have come as I promised," he said. Then he waved farewell and vanished.

Some nights, the past hovers over me as I gather up the loose ends of the day before dropping off to sleep. Gradually, almost imperceptibly, a form takes shape, lingering just long enough in my mind to ascertain the vague features of a man. He is an ill-defined presence so I can neither ascribe a name nor discern an intent. I think he may be a ghost come to watch over me or make amends. My chest aches as if pressed by a heavy hand. There is barely enough room to breathe. The ache reaches a critical mass, so deep and vast I fear it could swallow me whole.

13

False Summit

San Juan Mountains, September 1994: The closer I get, the more elusive the trophy. My destination today is farther than I think. It usually is. Optical delusion, as we mountaineers like to say. Chalk it up to oxygen deprivation or the blazing light at this altitude or overconfidence. After five solos in as many days, unscathed, I feel invincible.

When I top out on the summit ridge, the conquest appears imminent. The ridge before me curves like a hallucinated camel, rising to a distant hump that looks promising despite the modesty of its apparent cairn. I mop the sweat from my brow with my red bandanna, rehydrate with my half-empty water bottle, and push on. The cairn from the look of it up close has sat here undisturbed for centuries, the handiwork of a retreating glacier. On to the next hump. Splintered cumuli blister the azure sky. To the south and west, a sun-glazed tableau of unclaimed summits makes my heart race. I lick the stinging ooze from my windburned lip, relieve the friction in my right knee with a pop, and quicken the pace. The next hump fails to deliver the expected triumph, and the ridge beyond swaybacks to yet another high point. From there the ridge continues, on and on, over stacked and tossed plates of brittle shale that crack and crumble beneath my feet as I approach the next promising hump.

At first I mistake him for a lichen-splattered boulder, so deceptive is the pattern of his mottled fur. Head cocked, nose twitching, he seems to be enjoying the view while hunting for his next meal. Then the wind shifts slightly, driving my scent toward him. The white lining of a pointed ear rotates into view, an almond-shaped eye materializes.

Coyote, as close as I may ever get. He has a bald patch on his shoulder and a torn ear. A survivor, no doubt, of entanglements with barbed-wire fences and sheep guard dogs and all the other hazards of an often solitary, nomadic existence. The glint in his amber eye conveys a sly wisdom. Perhaps he will play me for a fool and warp my sense of direction with a ventriloquist's yelp so I never reach the summit. Maybe that's the point. There is no summit, just one step at a time, attending to what's under my feet.

Coyote squats on his haunches, unperturbed and inscrutable as a Buddha statue. And then, with the speed and sureness of a warrior's discharged arrow, he springs. I look over the edge, into steep, bottomless talus. He has vanished.

Twenty feet beyond his vacated perch is a pile of rocks arranged with human deliberation. Coyote has shown me the truest of seven false summits. In the triumph of the moment, our encounter is forgotten. How many false summits must I climb before I get the message and really start paying attention?

PART II

After the Fall

Mountains are there not to scale, but to teach.
They teach us how to find ourselves worthy
even when the world around us suggests that we are not.

—Jennifer Sinor

The bad news is you're falling through the air,
nothing to hang on to, no parachute.
The good news is there's no ground.

—Chögyam Trungpa Rinpoche

14

No Name Peak

Elk Range, July 4, 2000: I'm alone today. My camping companions departed at daybreak for Pyramid Peak, a pyramid of treacherous rock frequented by sudden storms. A peak I climbed in my impetuous, immortal youth. A sadomasochistic exercise if I were foolish enough to attempt the climb again with the undependable knees and declining eyesight of middle age. As Joe and Sam headed off in the opposite direction, I reined in my ambition, remembering the parting words of my therapist. "Listen to your body. It never lies."

Before setting off, Joe and Sam asked for a route description, and I mustered the best advice I could offer at the crack of dawn. Something about cairns, sudden shifts in wind direction and speed, and sensible judgment. Follow the cairns; they mark the safest route up. Pay attention to the relatively reliable barometer of the wind. If it picks up, changes direction, and blows in from the northwest, lightning may follow close behind, unloading its lethal cargo.

I worry most about Joe, an affable Mormon from Salt Lake City, who was the first to sign up for my Wasatch Mountain Club trip to Colorado's Maroon Bells Wilderness. He married young and has a devoted wife and two toddlers at home. This is his second fourteener in the Colorado Rockies. A successful ascent may give him the confidence to pursue the rest. In a tight spot, will his speed and enthusiasm overrule common sense? At his age I would have been chomping at the bit myself. At least he's wearing a red jacket, a trackable color.

I zip up my own jacket in anticipation of a chilly start and hoist my pack to its customary position. The fog in my sleep-deprived brain lingers until I'm high above our camp and squinting into the first rays of sun to touch the shoulders of Pyramid Peak. Farther up I come to a fork in the trail. Once the morning has brightened and warmed, a polyester-clad caravan will adhere to the main trail, passing by the alternative. I take the right-hand fork. It diverges from the named and mapped world we're accustomed to, which can lead to further estrangement, or wholeness and a kinder view of ourselves.

The sound of my breath whispering through my chest like static on a phone line suffices for company until I scare up three elk near the top of the pass. They bolt with a clatter into the basin where I am headed. On the other side of the pass, their scent disperses in marshes of June snowmelt carpeted in dry spots with bluebells, white bistort, and crimson king's crown. One sloppy footstep and I'll be wading knee high into frostbite. Nothing like solitude to discipline a rambling mind.

My destination is an unnamed peak, a faint triangle amid swirling contour lines on my topo map. Unlike the fifty-four fourteeners and the rest of the centennials, the tricentennials lack the stature and numbers of hikers to attract much notice from cartographers and guidebooks. To the half million peak baggers who march on the fourteeners each summer, they are practically invisible.

Once, while trekking up a high thirteener in the Mosquito Range, I looked back to see a trio in complementary Patagonia fleece trailing me up. "Your peak is over there!" I shouted, jerking my thumb at the fourteener across the ridge, swarming in hikers. They didn't believe me until I showed them my map. The tunnel vision of the quest blinded them, as it did me once, to other worthy ascents.

Anonymity has its benefits. Sometimes it is the most sensible choice. The elk can browse in relative peace, the wildflowers are less likely to be trampled to death, and I can hide out until the storm passes and it's safe to resume the journey.

I call today's destination No Name Peak. At least I'm not imposing a name—Mount Jane, for instance, or 285th Highest—overladen with ambition in an ostentatious bid for immortality. What if I were to approach the peak on its own terms, with an open mind, unhindered by categories and classifications, and let it dictate how the day will unfold? Easier said than done. For a reasonable shot at the summit, I must cross the basin and ascend one more pass, even less traveled than the first one. The peak's alternating layers of white and maroon shale keep me going, whetting my appetite with their resemblance to a birthday cake that has sat out in the sun too long. After several hours of nonstop hiking, the midmorning sun at my back, I'm feeling half-baked myself.

The basin conforms to the contours on my topo map, rising and falling in gentle, surmountable undulations, the high points jammed with boulders teetering above aquamarine pools. Some of the boulders could be elk. A fleet of cumulus sails across the basin, plunging it into flickering dusk, and then races toward Pyramid Peak where Joe and Sam are probably still making their way up. The storm could arrive in three hours or thirty minutes. I have less to worry about than they do; I can bail without a rope.

The next pass should deposit me on the summit ridge, provided my interpretation of the topo map is correct. The steep scree looks tedious, and I am grateful for the switchbacks of migrating elk and backpackers who have followed in their wake. A musky odor confirms my hunch that the elk have passed through here recently. I track their scent for a hundred feet or more before squatting to mingle my scat with theirs, steering clear of the skunk cabbage. The clouds have bloated into an armada of enemy ships. I have to make the pass before the storm does. From there, the summit will be within reach, a mere sprint.

It's going to take longer than I thought. Pinnacles of questionable rock force me off the ridge in favor of a less intimidating bypass. I forget about the gathering clouds, and my advice to Joe and Sam before we parted this morning, and concentrate on route finding. I forget until I'm sitting on the summit forty-five minutes later and gulping the contents of my second water bottle. If it takes me as long to return to the saddle as it did to reach the summit, I may be the loser in a neck-to-neck race with a lightning storm, and Joe and Sam will never sign up for another mountain club trip. Maybe I'm the one who should follow my advice of this morning.

Seventy feet back along the ridge, I stumble upon a breach in the cliffs. It drops me into a steep couloir, too steep for comfort. To my relief, the thundershower that kept me up half the night struck here as well, softening the gravel so the heels of my boots can dig in and apply the brakes, stabilizing my rocking body for the bumpy descent. I listen for the discharge of unmoored rock, the makings of a landslide that could upend me and sweep me down.

I am greeted at the bottom by the dark red pom-poms of king's crown waving in the wind. The queens are a daintier pink and none are in sight. Just an occasional king lording it over the bowing bluebells.

I take a long-overdue break atop the pass overlooking the trail to our campsite. Plunking myself down on the biggest stone mushroom in a trio, I rest my legs on the uppermost step of a talused terrace. Somewhere underneath, a pika squeals mightily for a critter I could cradle in the palm of my hand. The clouds have thinned into cobalt-tinged wisps. The restoration of summer or an intermission? I'm feeling optimistic. Sun-dazed and sleepy, I recline on my zabuton, letting the heat of the rock dissolve the spasms in my lower back. Above the basin, a raven trying to make headway in a sustained wind hits the pause button, tilting straight up on its tail as its wings freeze. Having encountered such conditions many times before without crashing to earth, it can be patient. Eventually the wind will lessen, and the raven will continue on its journey just as I must rouse myself from the hypnotic chanting of wind on rock and my fixation on the altar of triumphs from previous outings. To the south, Pyramid Peak juts above the chipped, rotten ridge to Thunder and Lightning Peaks. West of our campsite, the Maroon Bells stand side by side, the deadly traverse from north to south foreshortened of its actual hazards. Karl led the way, shepherding my entry into serious mountaineering. In the background, Lightning Peak's rolling contours belie the navigational challenges posed by its rubble-strewn approach. While most of my female colleagues were shuttling teenagers to soccer camp and catching up on their sleep, I was recalibrating my postmarital center of gravity on the junk rock of a lightning-prone thirteener.

I could lie here all afternoon in rapture, admiring the fruits of my labors, but I've got Joe and Sam to consider. They might appreciate a cup of hot tea after their climb, and a warm sleeping bag awaits me in a dry tent in the trees. If the storm materializes, that's where I should meditate—in a snug, sheltered tent.

I take one last gulp of water, doctor my chapped lips with sunscreen, tighten my bootlaces. As I stand up, a queen's crown emerges from beneath my right foot to display its pink blossoms, my first sighting of the season. The queen rebounds from the crush of my foot without losing any of the pink jewels in its crown. My foot delivered nowhere near the punishment of the ever-present wind. The queen withstands both by hugging the ground in a dense cluster of equally well-adapted flowers. In a kingdom as precarious as the tundra, there is no shame in deriving strength from the collective. It is an essential survival strategy, no less impressive than the location of the queen's ovules, tucked deep inside the carpels, beyond the reach of unwanted pollinators, insects that might cause irreparable harm. How to discriminate between desirable mates and deadly ones—I have to make those distinctions on my own.

My brain whirls with theories and speculations. In the sharp glare of the summer afternoon sun, it's hard to think straight, let alone see clearly.

Before lifting my pack and buckling in, I cup my hands to my eyes so I can scan the uppermost couloirs of Pyramid Peak for a glint of red. I finally spot Joe on the skyline ridge, looking again through squinting eyes to make certain the figure is not a mirage, a trick of the fierce light at this altitude. The spot remains motionless and congeals into a column of maroon rock. Wherever I look, I see no flickers of red to suggest movement or the final resting place of a fallen weekend warrior.

Red is the color of the soil that inspired the Spanish name of this state, of the Sangre de Cristos at sunrise and sunset. Hence their Spanish name, blood of Christ, shed for the redemption of sin, the blood of one supposedly atoning for all.

Red is the color of blood spilled over contested territory and competing claims. No territory is more contested than the territory of the besieged heart. Even when it surrenders, its narrowed arteries constrict the supply of oxygen.

I'm done with lists: the finished lists celebrated on champagne-soaked summits and the unfinished business that kept me awake at night. The centennials and bicentennials—counted like sheep as a sleeping draft until there were none, monuments now to a heroic odyssey. The tricen-whatevers, which at this precarious stage of life may never be completed. Fevered courtship letters from Karl and a letter from his bride, stuffed into the same drawer and nearly forgotten after one too many phone calls about the Bijou house. "Karl's obligations to you are through. You chose to live your lives separately. Please now allow us to live our life together uninterrupted." I left them all behind in Colorado with the rest of the junk I ditched when I moved to Utah in the fall of 1994 for a new job and fresh start. The file cabinet with my topo maps went with me in case I changed my mind about all those unclimbed peaks.

When I reach our campsite, I run into a member of another party attempting Pyramid Peak. He says he turned back. He didn't like the look of the weather. "No mountain is worth dying for."

15

Farther Off the Beaten Path

A fresh start means handing the key over to the couple renting Bijou and biting my tongue when the wife complains about the pale mauve exterior with evergreen and beige trim. "It's Victorian. It should be pink." It means keeping my eyes on the white dashes between my Honda Civic and the triple-trailer as the snowcapped mountains recede in my rearview mirror. I've crossed the border into Utah. I can't look back. I'll lose my nerve.

I'm giving up a sprawling city buffered by a fourteen-thousand-foot peak for a university town in a river valley hemmed in by slivers of Great Basin mountain range. In my former neighborhood of patchwork lots, dressed-up Victorians compete for attention with the brazenness of their three-toned color schemes. In Logan, the bland brick houses of Mormon pioneers are equally distributed across a symmetrical grid as if strict uniformity were a virtue.

Neighbors introduce themselves with loaves of homemade white bread, and I'm tossed back into seventh grade, trying to hold my own at the lunch table with a doughy mouthful of Wonder bread. It leaves an unsettling aftertaste. Conversations begin politely enough before invariably turning to "Where are your husband and children?" Not "Are you married? Do you have children?" But an assumption that excludes any other possibility. No one knows about the two hospitalizations, years of therapy, tit-for-tat infidelities, two hundred and seventy-eight scaled mountains. In Colorado I was just another divorcée panning for gold. In Utah my barren singlehood at age forty-three stands out like a white-feathered ptarmigan after the snow melts up high. Marriage and children gain admission to the celestial kingdom, where families procreate forever.

Everything about me—from my braless, skintight cycling attire to my unfettered speech and occasional overnight male houseguests—unintentionally flouts community standards. Exposed female flesh, premarital and extramarital sex and sex scenes at the movie theater, explicit references to one's buttocks, profanity blurted in the ill temper of the moment: guilty, guilty, guilty. The first time I pedal up Old Main Hill to campus, my boss, a native son welcomed back after making a name for himself in Washington, D.C., says, "I've never seen an adult woman on a bicycle before." When my computer screen blanks out, erasing weeks of work, I shout, "Jesus Christ!" The office goes eerily quiet. Flushed with shame, I vow never to make that mistake again. The censored magazine rack at the grocery store provokes unapologetic outrage. Scowling at *Parenting*'s cherubic toddler and *Family Circle*'s cherry-topped Bundt cake, both of which pass the purity test, I remove the brown plastic covers concealing the bare cleavages and shoulders on *Glamour* and *Vogue*. The cashier glares at me as if I had just hurled an insult or slapped her in the face. I don't care what she thinks. I want to see semiclothed women wallowing in the glory of their naked skin and sensuous curves, even though my curves are anything but. Uncovered, their partial nakedness will be so stunning, every man and woman in the store will stand at attention. And neither they nor their children or grandchildren will be tempted, as I once was, to lift a razor blade or finger in hatred.

The enormity of my culture shock drives me into the open arms of the no-Mos, the nickname for non-Mormons. At parties we pour ourselves glasses of wine and kick off our shoes and run off at the mouth, trying to locate ourselves in an inscrutable place. We're all in the same boat, rowing against the current. Outside, peering in. Annette, a rancher's daughter from Montana, misses the televised hockey games at her favorite brewpub in Bozeman, where obscenity-laced shouting matches broke out over whose team will win. Sofia from Santiago, Chile, wonders how she will teach Pablo Neruda's *Twenty Love Poems* after half the class walks out at the first mention of pubis. Judith, who was born in London and grew up in Albany, New York, can't understand why Utah Mormons call Jews gentiles. Her Orthodox grandparents were gassed at Auschwitz. "According to Mormonism, we're all gentiles," explains Annette, a pagan raised Methodist.

At the office I find common ground in our shock at a colleague's sudden, unexplained departure and in our delight in autumn's fiery reds and yellows as we rush upstairs to admire the peaking aspens and maples in the Wellsville Mountains. Even a surprise blizzard one early November morning joins us in commiseration over broken-down snowblowers and temporarily disabled backs. We had to shovel two feet of snow out of our driveways.

Fear of a violent home intrusion rarely crosses my mind, even though some nights my mattress rocks me awake more than once. If I die in my own bed, it will be at the hands of an earthquake, one of the hazards of living in northern Utah. In July, when the heat and mosquitoes become intolerable, I can depart for the Colorado Rockies without worrying about my house. I could leave the front door unlocked, the garage door open, and find nothing amiss on my return. The grass will be cut, a loaf of homemade white bread left inside the kitchen entryway.

My Mormon neighbors and colleagues are steeped in religion from birth. They wear it to work in modest dresses and white shirts with black ties, undergirded by sacred garments that declare their everlasting commitment. They proclaim their faith in prayers and hymns and testimonies on Sunday mornings, and again on Monday evenings at home, when they solidify their eternal family bonds with games and songs. Their faith scores winning touchdowns and determines their vote on Election Day and shields them in combat. Parents proudly give up their sons to the military and to two-year missions, sometimes in places where soldiers hesitate to go. If their sons are shipped home early, in coffins, they extol their sacrifice, comforted by the certainty of rejoining them in the next life, their bodies whole again.

My fellow no-Mos and I are well versed in the ways of the missionaries. Two clean-shaven men in black suits knock on the door, armed with a scripted pitch for our unaffiliated souls. Partly in self-defense I seek a community that resonates with my antiauthoritarian agnosticism, which clings to me years after abandoning my mother's Episcopalian heritage. Her church, to a rebellious adolescent in the early sixties, like a straitjacket of immobility and mortification with its hard pews, and kneeling and bowing and genuflecting, and recitations of the articles of faith. God, the maker of heaven and earth, whose judgment will surely rain down on me for telling my mother to go to hell after she grounded me for a month. The silent walk to the communion rail my last chance for redemption and a short-lived reprieve. I have to kneel again, bow my head. Jesus asleep on his crucifix, hanging from his pierced hands as I swallow the dry wafer and bitter wine of my mother's unwavering faith. Father Reinhart at the lectern on Palm Sunday, shaking the altar flowers with his booming voice; the choirmaster and parish secretary whispering in the vestibule after the announcement of his fatal car crash. "It wasn't an accident."

I'm doing my best to sit still—in a Buddhist Zendo in Salt Lake City, making myself as inconspicuous as possible in the back row of perfectly aligned cushions. Traffic rumbles through open windows. I cough, wiggle my numb foot, bracing myself for the ripple effect. Waves meet rock. How do my fellow meditators remain so resolute in their silent stillness? I return to my breath, as instructed, feeling an unexpected calm beneath the turbulence as my mind recycles the worn-out regrets, worries, and grievances it always has. But instead of participating in the Wild West show of my mind, my usual stance, confusing it with embodied experience, I sit, legs folded in half lotus, a spectator of Calamity Jane's misfortunes and comebacks. I didn't lose my mind when I ran away with a psychopath; I lost myself on the lawless frontier of my mind.

This realization holds me fast to my cushion even as my legs scream for release. I can do this. Just sit, with no agenda. I will count my breaths, if necessary, until the bell rings and I can finally stretch my legs before Genpo sweeps in, ocher-robed and bamboo staff in hand, to take his place up front.

Waving his staff at us, he says, "With your permission I'd like to hear from the damaged self."

I raise my hand. "I'm having a hard time with this one."

"Fear?" he suggests, holding my attention in the benevolent steadiness of his. Scanning the Zendo, he issues his next instruction. "Speak as the voice of fear."

He is taking us into the interior, to those places we can't bear to explore on our own. Unexamined, our minds run amok, wreaking havoc on our relationships with ourselves and others. The very thoughts on which we stake our identities are no more substantial or definitive than a puff of smoke. What we think is not what we are.

Fear. It churns in my belly, leaves a metallic flavor on my tongue, thins my breath, pulling it up to my throat. It turns me back before the storm turns deadly serious. It's the armor that deflects all arrows, lethal or harmless. What if I had understood this as a young woman? Tasted fear's myriad flavors so that I could recognize how tightly it had lashed me to my sister's mast.

I've sat before, with dedicated meditators who meet in a stuffy office above a busy restaurant. But Genpo seems to be the real deal, his teaching informed not only by the nearly eight centuries of patriarchs preceding him in Japanese Soto Zen but the insights of Western psychotherapy. He is a New York Jew who studied with a Japanese Zen master in southern California. His Zendo in Salt Lake City is packed with recovering Mormons and seekers from nearly every continent willing to sit in silence on behalf of their spiritual quest.

"There are mountains within mountains," Dōgen, the first patriarch, said. "Study them." And so we do.

Isabella Bird couldn't tolerate sitting still after her husband's death and two years of ill health and melancholy. When struck down before, she had picked herself back up with the only prescription that seemed to work. Set sail.

"It is a rather sad fact, but rough knocking about, open-air life, in combination with sufficient interest, is the one in which my health and spirits are the best," she wrote her publisher John Murray after testing the waters in 1888 with a five-week trip to Northern Ireland, where she investigated, for his magazine, the violent conflict between nationalists demanding independence and loyalists to the British Empire.

With her book royalties and inheritance, she could have settled for a comfortable life at home, shuttling among rented lodgings in Tobermory, a seaside village on the Isle of Mull, Edinburgh, and London, her domestic routine before her marriage and husband's death. Instead, she set sail again. For nearly half of the next twelve years, she traveled to some of the remotest regions on Earth, documenting her encounters with alien cultures in photographs and prose.

In India she established hospitals in memory of her husband and sister. That wasn't her only mission. But it was the mission that justified the rest of her itinerary without raising eyebrows about the sincerity of her self-abnegating evangelism. What she craved more than anything in the wake of her devastation, but would never admit to readers, was hardship, risk, and isolation. Tibet satisfied all three ambitions. Her caravan would have to cross the precipitous mountain passes of the Himalayas. The Buddhist prayer flags and shrines and monasteries constituted as alien a culture as one could hope for.

She never felt more alive than when her senses were magnified, sometimes to overly dramatic effect. The rain didn't just fall. It nearly swept her away in a downpour. The drifting snow buried her mule to its chest. The dangers were real. She nearly drowned with her horse during a perilous river crossing in Tibet. A one-thousand-mile journey across western Persia to the Black Sea began in one-hundred-degree heat and ended in a blizzard, her caravan repeatedly robbed by nomadic tribesmen. In China a mob of men chased her, the foreign devil, as her open chair was born through their village. Stones were thrown, knocking her unconscious. On that trip, of more than three years, she made certain to see Tibet again, where women enjoyed more freedom than anywhere else she had traveled, and the forested gorges and roaring rivers and views of Mount Everest and Kanchenjunga reminded her of the Colorado Rockies.

"I am far more at home in Tokyo and Seoul than in any place in Britain except Tobermory," she confessed in a private letter.

Despite her numerous ailments, she must have had the stamina of the yak that bore her over an eighteen thousand-foot pass in Tibet. Each time she returned home, it wasn't to rest or to commit the sin of idleness. She researched, wrote, and gave lectures. She met with the House of Commons and Prime Minister Gladstone. She was a sought-out authority on the far-flung conquests of the British Empire and its little-understood rivals. A woman with clout.

Her books had purchased a freedom few women of her time could conceive of. But after the death of her sister and husband, few traces could be found of the spontaneous Isabella who could admit to Rocky Mountain Jim's considerable charms. Facts and observations dominate the narratives of her books on Asia and the Middle East, as if she were trying to measure up to her male colleagues in the Royal Geographic Society. Looking inward might have brought her face-to-face with her grief.

"Five years," I promised myself when I departed for Utah. Friendships and the satisfactions of my work prolong my stay by five years, then ten.

A desert and a slew of mountain ranges separate me from the past. I no longer pose a threat to Karl's marriage. He has ceased to play the villain in my melodrama. We exchange Christmas cards and birthday wishes. He calls when his mother dies. She lay down for a nap after eating lunch and never woke up. His sobs cut me to the bone. He calls when his wife leaves him. I tell him how sorry I am, and I mean it. I know how much he hates to be alone. He says he's sorry, too, about everything. He doesn't have to explain. His tears are for both marriages.

In our world, families do not last forever. Nor do they configure by blood. We create them wherever we go, wherever we are, new attachments replacing vanished ones. My family includes the white-faced ibis nesting in the cattails and bulrushes of Cutler Marsh, the horned corals and fish scales and hard-shelled trilobites in Logan Canyon's limestone cliffs, the women faculty coffee club that meets at the artisan bakery, the foster child across the street.

She stands in my driveway, watching me push my mower back and forth across a quarter acre of weed-infested grass. I turn back toward the driveway and cut one last strip before letting go of the safety bar, which shuts off the motor.

"My brother mows the lawn. Why can't I mow the lawn?" she asks.

Next time I cut the grass, with her foster mother's permission, I place her hands on the crossbar below the handlebar and lean her against me to keep her out of harm's way. She in her long-sleeved, freshly ironed white shirt and pink pedal pushers; me in red shorts and black, spaghetti-strap tank top printed in white with "I've climbed 54 times over 14,000 feet."

I open the throttle, and squeezing the safety bar with one hand, pull the ripcord. The engine sputters to life. She squeals with delight. Her brother is watching from their front porch. The mower shakes and rattles and wiggles forward. "If it hits a rock, Loreen, it could kick back on us so hang on to the crossbar."

I wrap my arms around her as I push the mower along, bracing her with my stomach in case she stumbles backwards. Every girl deserves at least one chance to cross the Continental Divide.

16

Extremity

Summer 2002: I could spend the rest of my life in Utah and never stop calling the Colorado Rockies home. They gave birth to the woman I am today. At each dizzying crux, the mountains were the one anchor in my life that held. The anchor still holds when I tumble into the loneliness and confusion of expatriatism. Memories leap to my rescue, catching me before I hit bottom. My sister Alice and I discharging our cabin fever in a Neverland of fantasy play far removed from parental preoccupations. The roar of Ruxton Creek at the height of spring runoff, as soothing a decade after the divorce as when I lay in bed wondering what my tardy husband was up to. The infinitesimal sweep of geologic time at my feet as I stand atop a summit cairn and contemplate the never-ending creation story of a continent in constant, imperceptible flux. The humble span of one incomplete lifetime weighed against three hundred million years of mountain building, erosion, and reemergence.

I don't have to take a geology course to notice how the veins in my hands and in a shale formation in the San Juan Mountains are cut from the same cloth, which inspires a story for the university magazine about a paleontologist who revives the extinct fishes of the Eocene with the murals he creates out of his fossil excavations.

At the Zendo in Salt Lake City they tell us to drop our stories and engage wholeheartedly with every moment of our precious lives. But what if our stories don't really belong to us and they're simply messengers for the voiceless and unheard? I have never lived among wolves or herded cattle on the open range, but I have seen enough coyote pups and kills in the Colorado Rockies to write with conviction and fair-mindedness about a cattle ranch in Montana trying to coexist with wolves. Perhaps this story will persuade some fifth-generation rancher to reconsider the zero-tolerance policy of his pioneer ancestors. I have a hearty respect for the wind, born of firsthand experience with its endless capacity for invigoration and violence, and that respect underlies every paragraph about a wind energy farm in Wyoming supplying electricity to southern California and a rancher $50,000 per year in royalties. Will the story lessen some of the resistance to sustainable energy as an alternative to our suicidal addiction to fossil fuels? Who knows? Maybe I'm delusional. But I keep writing stories in hopes they will go out into the world and stand on their own two feet and shake up the status quo.

The Colorado Rockies burn brightly across the miles of separation, grounding my stories in the bedrock of memory. But in my dreams they are frozen in a distant ice age, covered from head to toe in glaciers, their ridgelines corniced and teethed with icicle daggers. The glaciers sprawl across the tundra, broken up by bottomless crevasses. The shiny surface of a lake raises hope of a route across. I climb into a boat and start rowing, but the lake is frozen, too, and choked with impassable icebergs. I turn back. I will never find a way through.

Come July I will go home—to hike with friends and rendezvous with my parents. My Honda Civic is so loaded down with topo maps and camping gear, the rear bumper scrapes blacktop when I back out of the driveway.

The icescape of my dreams is no more disorienting than the death-scape that confronts me as I drive across Trail Ridge Road to spend a week with my parents in Estes Park. This year the snow melted two months early. The rain never came. Landmarks as familiar and comforting as the storybooks of my childhood look otherworldly, tottering on the brink of extinction because of a rapidly warming climate. Aquamarine ponds humming with birdsong in previous summers have shriveled into mummy's skin. Snowfields where Alice and I pelted each other with snowballs have melted back to gravel. At the crest of the road, I stop at the Alpine Visitor Center and hike up into the tundra overlooking Fall

River Cirque. Stunned by the silence, I listen for sounds of life other than the crunch of my boots on grasses as sharp as sewing needles. Just as I will listen, with an even more desperate longing, on my arrival at the condo, for Dad's gagging cough. It would signify he's upright, awake, if not conversant. His hearing too compromised, his mind too cluttered perhaps for him to offer more than a smile.

We dare not leave the condo without face masks even though they are worthless. After several years of ever-diminishing precipitation, wildfires have broken out across the state. Smoke fills valleys, towers into clouds twenty thousand feet high, drifts into Wyoming and Nebraska. The Hayman fire in the Tarryalls, on the southwestern tip of the Front Range, has combusted into the biggest wildfire in Colorado history. A satellite image shows a smoking black fist clenched over four counties. The lucky ones manage to toss armloads of prized possessions into the back of their SUVs before fleeing the whirling dervishes of destruction that will torch their homes to their foundations. The fires burn so hot, pyrocumulus clouds form, racing toward Denver at fifty miles per hour, assaulting residents with the equivalent of two-to-five years' worth of industrial emissions.

When Mother and I finally venture out for a picnic at our favorite overlook on Trail Ridge Road, we search in vain for Longs Peak. The haze has reduced the peak to a grainy mass of gray in a contracted panorama. This could be Alice's perspective, and mine of her, after forty years of hospitalization, and group home and county nursing home care. Perhaps the wrinkled postcard of Longs Peak on her dresser prompts a memory of family vacations. Whenever I visit, I bring a new card and ask, "Remember our picnics on Trail Ridge Road?"

Our hopes dashed of seeing the peak, and acutely aware of Alice's absence, Mother and I have lost our appetites. I pack up the sandwiches. Despite our face masks, invisible embers sting our throats and eyes. Coughing and tearing up like unrepentant chain smokers, we can retreat to our condo for the rest of the day and nurse our sore throats with Listerine. The elk have no such recourse. The emaciated survivors straggle down the highway and into Estes Park single file, a trail of shed fur marking their route. With no food up high, they're scavenging for roots in denuded lawns and gardens. Usually we see whole herds grazing on the front lawn of the Stanley Hotel and golf course below. Not this year.

This year we spend much of the week in front of the TV, mesmerized by the military might of the counterattack, praying for the inferno to end. Air tankers douse burning foothills in red retardant, which blooms into sickening reminders of the chemically defoliated jungles of the Vietnam War. Hotshot crews shovel and hose to beat back flames advancing on private property. Risking their lives after decades of misguided public policy that equated wildfire with Armageddon instead of a rejuvenating force of nature. For eons lightning-sparked fires thinned the forests, creating the conditions for seedlings to take root. With fewer fires to regulate their health and density, trees have multiplied, packed in so tightly, they extinguish the sunlight. And all the ills of overpopulation—from disease and insect infestations to overgrown underbrush—accumulate. Choked forests manufacture the fuel for the tossed cigarette or muffler spark to ignite; the warmer temperatures and extreme droughts and winds of climate change fan the flames, stretching the fire season and resources to combat it to the breaking point.

At night the fires die down, smoldering in the underbrush, until the shooting spree restarts next morning. Sparks fly into treetops, where they burst into exploding cannonballs that jump from crown to crown. Ancient trees that thrived in the self-regulating wildfire regimen of previous centuries are defenseless, their lofty groves incinerated into graveyards of charred stumps.

Forgoing our usual drives to view the elk in Horseshoe and Moraine Parks, we accompany Dad on his daily errands to the relatively safe, smoke-free grocery store. Once-steady hands with a sure grip jerk the steering wheel with alarming regularity. Mother and I keep the conversation going without raising the obvious question. What's with Dad? Having given up Scotch and soda thirty years ago with the help of Alcoholics Anonymous, he now downs cocktails of prescribed pills. At home, his pharmacy spills out of his vanity onto his bathroom sink. It treats a dim constellation of complaints, only a handful of which I can name. I watch his trembling hands on the wheel, my growing, unarticulated unease trapped beneath the surface in a layer of permafrost. His hands, a harbinger of doom like the rainclouds after the Hayman fire. Residents downstream prayed for rain throughout the drought years. Now they watch the sky with dread. A cloudburst could unleash a flood of mud and debris from blistered slopes stripped of their protective coating of trees.

Two summers later, in another foreshadowing of what's in store with climate change, the pendulum swings to the other extreme, as though compensating for the austerity years. The Colorado Rockies have seen monsoons and droughts before, but these storms hunker down with sullen tenacity, the rain falling with such blinding fury that it washes away mountainsides and sweeps cars off roadways. Once the saturated soil dries out and the mist burns off, the meadows and panoramas of my childhood throb with the green intensity of Isabella Bird's Scottish Hebrides.

We celebrate with a family picnic at Hollowell Park. As far as I can tell, not one splinter remains of Fred Bowen's cabins. Time and asphalt and a towering forest have seen to that. On the lee side of the parking lot, ponderosas soar above our picnic table, enveloping us in welcome shade. After our picnic, we park Dad on the bench nearest the latrine, where there are no trees to block our view of him. "We won't be long," Mother promises.

I want to show her the meadow where Alice and I played. Mother hasn't seen it in years. The elk rarely make an appearance in broad daylight, and today is no exception. Beaver-dammed marshes dense with willows have encroached on their evening pasture, where Alice and I created a royal court out of wildflowers. Despite its altered appearance, the meadow endures, its place in our family lore magnified by the ethereal light of an Albert Bierstadt painting. The glow extends to Mother's face, softening the wrinkles and worry lines. A blizzard of white specks flickers across the ankle-deep grass. The meadow is exhaling clouds of white cabbage butterflies. They adorn our hair, our chests, our bare, intertwined arms.

We shouldn't leave Dad alone for long. He could wander off or forget Mother's instructions, forget we're returning soon, and start shouting, "Jane! Mary! Where are you? Jane! Mary! Mary!" And there would be another scene—with park rangers and tourists rushing to his aid instead of the security guards and shoppers who respond to his panic-stricken confusion at the mall in Kansas City. His sense of direction nowhere near as reliable as our first trips to Colorado when he would set off in our Ford woody, exploring the park without asking for directions, after glancing at his atlas or one of the half dozen maps in the glove compartment.

I'm the designated driver now. Dad finally has a diagnosis: Parkinson's. It not only explains the shaking hands, but the coughing fits; shuffling, labored gait; sudden stops and starts. At first we accept these changes as if they are just another variation in an idiosyncratic personality. But as the months and years pass, he freezes up without warning, in midsentence or action, still recognizably Dad but inanimate as a wax figure in a museum. This is what convinced Mother and me to assume his place behind the wheel. If his right foot were to stomp on the accelerator, like it has in Kansas City, immovable in the face of imminent catastrophe, he could drive us right off a cliff. Or if the needle of a random thought got stuck, repeating itself like a refrain from a gospel hymn, he might lose his bearings altogether and let go of the wheel, having forgotten where he is.

With a tight grip on Mother, whose balance is tentative because of her arthritic spine and knees, I head back to the parking lot. The smell of melting tar on the sunny side of the lot attests to the heat of the early-afternoon sun. The bill on Dad's baseball cap has slipped over his glasses and is resting on the tip of his Teutonic nose. His Rand McNally atlas has fallen out of his lap. If he weren't dozing, he would be flipping the pages with a dazed look, orienting himself to a pastime in which he can no longer partake.

I pick up the atlas and straighten his baseball cap. His dazzled blue eyes open wide. "You're the prettiest gals on the planet," he exclaims, as if seeing us for the first time.

Back at the condo, Mother confesses, "I can't do it again. Six hundred and fifty miles. Dad shouting half the time. The traffic from Denver to Estes. This is our last trip." Worn out by the caretaking, she sold their home of forty years and auctioned off everything but the essentials and heirlooms that their apartment at the senior village could accommodate. Consigned to the estate sale were the railway timetables and maps with which Dad would plot his course across the western United States and Canada. Fantasy trips planned in the comfort of his recliner, the chattering TV an uncritical source of encouragement.

As the Parkinson's sucks him further and further into an alternate reality, where space–time expands and contracts and bends with stupefying randomness, suspending him in an arrested free fall, the resemblance to Alice becomes ever more noticeable, not just the seemingly unbridgeable vastness of their disconnection from us, but their insatiable hunger.

On my biannual visits to Kansas City, soon after we bring Alice home for the afternoon from the county nursing home where she will probably spend the rest of her life, I find Alice and Dad fast asleep in their adjacent chairs in his bedroom. A Nebraska Cornhuskers game proceeds without them, the babble of the TV commentators falling on deaf ears. Dad's extra-large golf shirt is spotted with apple and carrot bits from his frequent, surreptitious raids of the refrigerator. "I'm going to put a lock on it," Mother mutters as she spies the incriminating fingerprints on the door handle that must be sponged off—again. The stains on Alice's triple-X lavender pullover, easily mistaken for stab wounds, elicit a resigned shrug of the shoulders. Mother knows the source all too well. It's ketchup from the uncapped bottle Alice empties onto the french fries they regularly serve at the nursing home.

Undaunted by mealtime messes, Mother heats up a can of Campbell's tomato soup. The scent of it simmering on the stove rouses Dad and Alice out of their nap, into heightened-alert mode as if their team had just scored the winning touchdown. "Lunch?" Alice inquires.

"Ten more minutes, Alice. Mother has a salad to prepare."

Dad pats his breast pocket, the storage bin for the spoon he took from the utensil drawer and the M&M's he snatched from the candy dish on their neighbor's doorway shelf. Alice opens her purse and pulls out the unwashed coffee mug that accompanies her everywhere outside the nursing home. "Would you like a cup of coffee, Jane?"

"No thanks. I don't drink coffee."

"I want a cup of coffee, Jane."

"You just had one. Let's wait until after lunch."

"A cup of coffee, Jane. I'd like a cup of coffee."

After lunch, I supervise so Mother can take a rare break in the exercise room upstairs. The refrigerator door opens and shuts five times in twenty minutes. I race into the kitchen in time to catch the culprit red-handed as a chunk of dried-up cheese enters the worn grinder of Dad's mouth. The candy and cutlery collection in his breast pocket now includes a chocolate Oreo cookie and a second spoon.

"Dad, that's your fifth snack since Mom left for the exercise room."

"Snack? I'm hungry. I haven't eaten in hours."

"Dad, you just ate lunch."

"No, I didn't." He proclaims his innocence with a hand over his heart. His yellow golf shirt acquires several rows of red and blue polka dots as the crushed M&M's in his breast pocket melt.

"Dad!"

He disarms me with a giggle that exposes his recessed upper gum. Alice pads into the kitchen in her bare feet and flashes a toothless grin as she holds up her coffee mug. "Coffee, Jane? Make me a cup of coffee." Their laughter jiggles every ounce of their abundant flesh. I burst out laughing, too. Shameless, unselfconscious laughter. The joke is on all of us, and for once I welcome my inclusion.

I could be wearing an upside-down salad bowl on my head with spinach in my teeth, and they couldn't care less. Social niceties and feminine propriety matter less than just this, a moment of uncensored togetherness.

It's time to drive Alice back to the nursing home. Dinner is all she can think about. I reach into Dad's pocket and straighten his spoons as Alice puts on her jacket.

"You're the prettiest girls on the planet," Dad says, pressing two fingers to his lips to blow us a kiss.

After the Care Center takes over full time, reanimating him with its bingo games and sing-alongs and chair exercises, he notes our arrivals and departures with the same ritual. It is the only line and gesture in his script he can perform from memory. For the rest of our visit, he asks the same question over and over.

"Is this Tuesday?"

"Yes, it's Tuesday."

Thirty seconds later: "Is this Tuesday?"

"Yes, Tuesday."

The moment the door automatically locks behind us, he forgets we were there. The demands of the ever-present now consume past and future.

It is six in the morning Kansas City time when Mother calls on the nurse's cell phone. She says Dad's face is turned toward the window beside his bed and the rising sun, a propitious direction for leave-taking, according to Tibetan Buddhists.

"He looks so young. Not one wrinkle." In the background a passing train wails. "It's carrying him off," she whispers.

His cremation consoles me. Fire suppressed roars back with a frightful vengeance. How long-lived and far-reaching the destruction only time will tell. But fire, as Tibetans understand it, purifies both body and mind. Our physical form dissolves into sheer luminescence. Our mental confusions transmute into wisdom.

In October, after most of the tourists have gone home and the elk have ventured down to conduct their mating rituals, I will scatter my share of Dad's ashes in the meadow at Hollowell Park. To assist his passage, I will visualize, in my farewell meditation, a flock of butterflies escorting him on his journey. His passage secured, the father of my youth will resurrect in memory, gripping the wheel once again to steer us confidently into adventure, as Alice shouts, "Fifteen more miles!" at the top of her lungs and the Little Thompson River froths at the banks, straining against the confinement of its sinuous canyon.

17

Pinned Again

San Juan Mountains, July 2007: The boulder is the tallest obelisk in a field of tabletop-size stones, seemingly undisturbed by the passage of centuries. If this were Mexico, it could have borne witness to a human sacrifice at Teotihuacan. I wish I had a camera.

I must have brushed the boulder with my right elbow as I looked back to check on Jake. It happens so quickly. Inhale, exhale, a turn of the head. I hear an ominous rasp. The boulder is moving, and suddenly I'm on my back—flailing, drowning in a tsunami of pain—my right leg caught below the knee in a tightening vise. My calf is pinned between two boulders, the one that just tipped over and the one underneath.

Suppressing a scream, I sit up and push. The boulder doesn't budge. I push again, encouraged by a shudder of lessening resistance. The vise responds with a nauseating squeeze. I lean back, pressing my buttocks into the boulder underneath to maximize my leverage, and ram the boulder on top with a hip and shoulder butt. The rebound knocks me flat, and the boulder bears down, crushing more calf muscle.

I could hear Jake's curses below me as I scrambled up the chimney to the summit ridge. He had to duck to dodge some flying pebbles. Can he hear my shrieks now? We hooked up via Match.com, and this is the first serious test of our compatibility in the mountains. Somewhere in the maze of gullies between the summit and me, he is making his way down in running shoes with no ankle support, a cliff below him if he slips on the loose rock.

My other companion, Arlene, a speed demon of a mountaineer from Salt Lake City, has long since disappeared over the rise below, probably clocking her pace with her watch as she sprints for the car. Will my shrieks reach her? My throat clenches, overcome by the strain. With every muscle in my chest I force the screams out into our mountainous echo chamber. Surely they can hear me now. Precious minutes pass. I'm trapped, my calf slowly and surely being crushed to death. Where the hell are they? We shouldn't have strayed so far apart. Clawing at the boulder, I plead for help, shout every obscenity I know. I refuse to be silent. I will fight for my leg, my right to be whole.

The click, click, click of advancing hiking poles announce Jake's rapid approach. Panting, he drops his poles, kneels beside the boulder, and shoves with all his might. The boulder tilts toward me. I curse in three languages and wail from the pain, the panic. Arlene arrives and kneels by my side, helpless as I flop on my back, exhausted by the pain and futility of a one-sided wrestling match. The slightest movement on my part increases the pressure on my leg. Arlene barely weighs one hundred pounds—a lightweight in a contest against a ton of quartzite. We are three-and-a-half miles from the car, two thousand seven hundred vertical feet. It will be dusk by the time my companions hit the road, hours after sunrise before a search and rescue team can reach me. The steep, rocky, wind-raked terrain rules out a helicopter landing.

Jake studies the position of the boulder from every conceivable angle. Then he squats as if competing again in a collegiate wrestling match. Relying on the laws of physics rather than blunt force, he braces himself with his muscular thighs, hugs the boulder tight, and pushes with his arms and chest. The boulder gives slightly, shifting in the right direction until finally, at last, there is just enough space to drag my leg out. I roll up my bloody pant leg, expecting to see snapped fibula. No bone protrudes. But my calf has swelled into a grotesque mutation of its usual shape. I feel nothing below the knee, nothing at all, even where the skin is ripped and bleeding. I swallow a Percocet from Arlene's first aid kit and another from Jake's, and they get me up on my left leg. Leaning on their shoulders, I hop on my good leg across the rest of the boulder field, to the snowfield below. They pack some snow in my rain jacket and wrap the jacket around my calf.

I limp out on the crutches of my friends' shoulders. Three hours later they bundle me into the back of Jake's pickup for the one-hour drive to Lake City and the only medical clinic within fifty miles.

Next morning an orthopedist in Gunnison examines the X-rays. "Lucky you. No broken bones. One inch higher and I'd be scheduling a knee reconstruction with plates, screws, and a bone graft. An inch lower and I'd be reconstructing your ankle joint. With that much metal in your body, you wouldn't clear airport security without triggering the alarm."

"My leg was under that boulder for no more than fifteen minutes. How long could it have withstood so much weight?"

"Hard to say. An hour maybe. Then we'd be scheduling surgery for sure."

He shows me, with a pinch of my big toenail, how to check for impaired circulation, a side effect of massive swelling that could result in gangrene, amputation, kidney failure. "If the nail doesn't turn pink within five seconds, or if you have any chest pains, go straight to the emergency room. A blood clot could kill you."

Bloated beyond recognition, cut and badly bruised but unbroken, my crushed calf seems symptomatic of an emotional injury in dire need of attention.

That night I sleep under the sequined black velvet of the night sky, my right leg propped on Jake's spare sleeping bag. Now that climbing season has come to a premature end, I contemplate the future with a mixture of curiosity and dread.

Home again in Utah, I shuffle across campus with the aid of a borrowed walker. Two weeks later I graduate to a cane. Colleagues urge me to take a break and stay home—an exceptional departure from routine. I'm teaching full time now in a small department, and my students, who take two to three classes from me before graduating, arouse a latent maternal instinct. They seek help with their homework and career advice, and consolation after a breakup or the death of a family member.

Reluctantly, I take my colleagues' advice and stay home for a week. My right calf imprisoned in ice, I can't sit still on my meditation cushion, my refuge during emotional upheavals. Unable to hike, I grow increasingly homesick for my mountains. Mine, as if my dedication and devotion entitled me to possession.

I miss the purposefulness of the climb. Even the pain serves a larger purpose. Five miles may feel like fifty at times, but without the gravitational force of blisters, bruised shins, scraped knuckles, and throbbing knees to hold me fast, my mind might detach and float away.

If not in motion, in physical contact, how else can I keep body and mind from flying apart? Petrify my brain on the sediment of *Family Feud, Judge Judy, The Young and the Restless*? I have no desire to repeat the mind-numbing escapism of my housewife years. And, despite the temporary setback of the accident, I'm too content with my life to dye my hair orange in protest of the injustices of aging. Having run out of ideas, I consult my library of self-help books. *The Wisdom of Menopause.* I have my doubts. What nuggets of wisdom can be plucked out of my hot flashes and memory lapses of late? *There Is Nothing Wrong with You* (Revised Edition). I've been reconfiguring my narrated self my entire adult life, excavating and excising the hidden defects that complicate *Getting the Love You Want* and *Keeping the Love You Find.* Since moving to Utah, I've had two boyfriends in six years, dependable and monogamous—progress, to be sure. Mother was visiting when Larry emailed his Dear Jane on our first anniversary. As I collapsed in a heap of despair, she tried to comfort me. "Maybe you're trying too hard to rectify what went wrong in your marriage. Maybe he's afraid he can't live up to your expectations." Arnie made the ninety-mile commute from his place in Salt Lake to mine in Logan so he could tell me in person. This time I wasn't surprised. He was an uncompromising atheist, and I meditate at the Zen Center so I can disengage from the internal dialogue that quarrels over every aspect of my life with suffocating irresolution.

One night, teetering on hopelessness, I decide to study the topography of my own body, the body I divorced before an unjust emergency room tribunal and seek to reclaim on every ascent in hopes of a lasting reconciliation. Darkness is my ally, the prying eyes of my self-consciousness appeased with shut blinds and switched-off lights and a blanket draped over my naked body. Closing my eyes, I delegate the exercise to the sensation of touch. Unlike previous explorations supercharged with urgency, my hands wander all over, with no destination or objective. Just flesh and bone and muscle. The texture of eroding skin; the strength of well-exercised buttocks and thighs; the mica-smooth belly; the flat, firm breasts elevated into soft mounds by the cleft in my rib cage. Parting the flesh with my fingers, I let them slide across the saddle of my pelvis, toward the wilderness. I approach this strange, fearful terrain with the awkward tentativeness of my first climb on Mount Sherman, my first date with Will. The safest approach, the patient one favored by mountaineers who have learned from experience not to charge straight at the summit.

If we sit still often enough and really listen, Genpo's successor says, our judgments about ourselves will wane, and we'll stop treating ourselves as lifelong self-improvement projects, as sinners in need of constant redemption. I may not be able to sit still while recovering, but I can listen. My body speaks in a language I scarcely know. It speaks with raw sensation, with fire and ice, sharp edges, and a spaciousness encompassing the whole universe.

My body doesn't want to be conquered; it wants to be cherished. Such a conversation cannot be rushed or forced. Even that modest of an undertaking would have been unthinkable for Isabella Bird. A woman's body was so dangerous perhaps, not only to the social order but to herself, it had to be concealed in dense fabrics and petticoats, restrained in corsets to the detriment of her health. Abroad, in the untrammeled wilderness, Isabella could give free reign to the barely permissible. In her responses to landscape I glimpse moments of religious ecstasy, a substitute perhaps for passion. "Floods of golden glory." "Rose-lit summits." "The land nearer now in all its grandeur, gaining in sublimity." Bound for Longs Peak on horseback, the gloomy forest lit here and there with yellowing aspen leaves as Rocky Mountain Jim regaled her with stories, she might have allowed herself to feel desire.

Six weeks after the accident, I'm back on the trail, testing my leg to see how steep an incline, how much mileage it can bear. Now I have two dents—the one in my sternum noted by my mother's obstetrician at birth and the one in my calf delivered by a mountain.

Despite the scar tissue, my calf is surprisingly flexible. If I push too hard, though, a dull, persistent ache takes hold, infusing me with caution.

Sometimes what we love harms us, a wise woman once told me. And a beautiful endeavor takes a terrifying turn. I keep climbing because after thirty years of mountaineering, I have more faith than ever not only in my orienteering skills but also in the journey. Held flat and steady—the red side of the needle aligned with magnetic north and the declination on the map accounted for—a compass will get me where I want to go. Where am I headed? I haven't the faintest idea. Eventually I will arrive somewhere and there will be a good story to tell. As for those passersby who tease me—"Did you get kicked by a moose?"—I take no offense. My encounter with the boulder provides a cautionary tale. Do not hike off trail alone.

18

Homecoming

Mosquito Range, July 2012: The coyotes serenade me with their nocturnal flutes as I lay awake, too agitated by the locomotive of Jake's snoring to fall asleep. It's astonishing how much I can accomplish in one restless night. I mount a rigorous defense and summation of the evidence acquitting me of the shame of unemployment. Eight million Americans lost their jobs in the meltdown of the Great Recession. If not for my early retirement and the real estate bust, my return to Colorado would have been delayed by work obligations and unaffordable housing.

It's not the triumphant return I had envisioned—thanks to my decimated savings—but here I am nonetheless, twisting my sleeping bag into knots, as I argue my case before a hostile jury of my own imagining. After laying that case to rest, I rehearse and re-rehearse a tender change-of-heart scene with an ex-lover that will never be performed live. He retired and lives in a tepee in Montana and juggles three girlfriends simultaneously without their knowledge. For once I don't get mad when the dog barks back at the coyotes. His barking interrupts the insistent momentum of my thinking.

I had no desire to own another dog, not as a single woman in Mormon country with long-distance-only dating prospects, but after liberating him from an outhouse where some Good Samaritan had housed him to prevent him from dashing onto the roadway, I couldn't bear to leave him, a half-starved feral mutt, at the mercy of the mountain lions or to some other gruesome fate. I named him Beast in hopes of transforming him into a beauty. For a runt dumped in the mountains, he soon blossomed with obedience training into a faithful hiking companion. In his youth he would take off—a hurtling marvel of strength, balance, and coordination; a dark speck flying toward the summit. He still makes the summit before I do, waiting by the cairn until my gasping arrival. Now that we share the same arthritic complaints, we step gingerly around and over obstacles, conserving our energy with a rational pace.

So when Beast howls back at the coyotes half an hour before our customary wake-up call from Nan, our drill sergeant for the past six summers, I remind myself of our mutually beneficial relationship, a kinship born of deformity, abandonment, and recovery.

Beast's barking not only startles Jake out of a sound sleep, it relieves Nan of her self-appointed duty to bugle our lazy butts out of our bags so we can hit the trail early enough to avoid the afternoon thundershowers.

Soon after our departure, the sun appears, dousing the shaded willows and wildflowers in a rainbow of color. The yellow flower heads of the old-men-of-the-mountain open, dish-antenna-like, as Nan and Jake resume the debate I abandoned at dawn. Whose control freak of a boss is the bigger pain in the ass? Whose profession, in the wake of recession-driven budget cuts, serves as the easiest target for elimination? Their commentary persists as we hike up the closed mining road, through willow-clogged marshes, to the knoll overlooking the collapsed remains of a miner's shack in the narrow basin below the pass. They both merit sympathy—Nan for the impossible productivity mandates that compromise the quality of her care for indigent clients, Jake for the demoralizing mismatch between numbers and preparation of students and the all-or-nothing stakes of standardized testing. So they hike and they hike, grinding their frustration into dust. Me, too, at times. My career in higher education is over, not by choice, but because of a combination of circumstances that has driven thousands of instructors out of the profession.

As the mountain nears, spongy hummock switches to steepening talus. Nan and Jake charge up without looking back, hell-bent on the summit, receding into rock, then nothingness. Beast chases after them, preferring to be at the head of the pack. When I finally catch up, Nan and Jake are packing up their cameras and windbreakers in preparation for the descent. Soon they're clattering down, enjoying the vigorous challenge of the competition. Before the accident I would have happily participated. At the bottom of the steep talus, they spot a shortcut, which crosses a boulder field before diving into a rocky, willow-infested trench. Foolhardy terrain for my grinding arthritic knee. Every other step a jitterbug with pain. So I go my own way and retrace the lengthier, more forgiving route of this morning, while Beast runs back and forth, undecided, until he tires of the unnecessary round-trip mileage and stays with me as I cross the upper basin.

The old-men-of-the-mountain have pivoted to collect the heat of the early afternoon sun. The silver roof of the crumpled miner's shack shines like aluminum foil amid the chaos of scattered shingles and siding, rusted nails and iron pipes. The tundra reclaims what it can. Blue bells drape their chimes over the slats of a broken bedframe. Alpine avens stitch the scraped soil back together with their green foliage and yellow blossoms. Beyond the shack the rutted road begins, looping around to the edge of the moraine, then down into the far side of the lower basin. An egg-shaped boulder perches above the more direct descent into the heart of the basin. This is my route.

Even though I've hiked this basin before, I have to search for breaks in the willows that might go all the way through. Sometimes an opening appears, which serpentines into another opening without dropping me to my hands and knees. Other times I have to back out and look elsewhere for an alley that doesn't dead-end. Usually the dog and I stick to the same musky, intermittent pathway of the elk. Once in a while we separate as he thrashes through a pocket too tight for humans. As in life, progress is best measured on a quantum scale. The journey is rarely straightforward and only becomes clear afterward. We put one foot in front of the other and keep going, not to get somewhere necessarily, but for the journey itself. As long as we keep moving, and do not succumb to panic (or fall into a hidden mine shaft), we'll make it out by nightfall. We're in no danger of dying, even though we may think we are.

Ahead, a rock outcropping promises an exit strategy. The sporadic pathway reappears as it climbs out of the willows and angles around the outcropping, paralleling the winding, muddy creek channel below until it has nowhere to go but down into the muck. The channel narrows and deepens. We're bashing in and out of willows again, Beast's swishing black-and-white tail blazing the way forward. We're immersed in willows, whipped into submission by their dangling, scrambled branches. Beast's tail slips under an impassable clump, and that's the last I see or hear of him. I have no idea where he is. Branches slap me in the face, tear at my bare forearms and shins. I stumble, almost falling to my knees. My left foot has stepped into a depression and caught on a branch. Another bigger branch wiggles across my right foot, catapulting me face-first into a mound of fur. Beast is lying on his belly, tugging on the branch that entrapped my left foot. The branch has a tiny, heart-shaped hoof. It is attached to the slender leg of a newborn fawn. She must be dead. Her leg is in Beast's mouth. He licks it with a look of curiosity rather than murderous appetite. Fair game or not, it's a sacrilege to disturb the dead.

Crying out, I scoop up the fawn and hug her to my chest. Beast lunges. Holding the fawn with one arm, I seize him by the collar with my free hand so I can jerk him away. Maybe she died in the night and her mother left to rejoin the herd. I cradle her with both arms. She is light and limp as a silk scarf. I roll her upward into a tighter embrace, against my heart, and then I feel it. A tiny heartbeat races double time against mine, thumping like frantic, gloved knocks on the door. Beast thrusts his snout in close so he can sniff her hind legs. She is so small and fragile and helpless, I must protect her, my only weapon the leash I fashion with my shirt. I yank hard, separating them. Beast breaks free and burrows into her white rump. I block his next lunge, jostling the inert bundle in my arms. The fawn opens her eyes and bleats. Not dead, but very much alive. Her mother may be watching from her hiding place in the willows, having picked up our scent before we stumbled onto the nest. Watching and waiting for us to disappear so she can retrieve her newborn. This is what I want to believe, grasping for assurance when there is none. If only I could press rewind and reroute this scene. If only I could return the fawn to her nest so her mother could reclaim her. But that would put her in harm's way again. On the other side of the trough, more willows crowd the bank. I make a break for them, desperate for any shelter that might shield her from the dog. She squirms and kicks with an astonishing ferocity for such a delicate, lightweight creature. I hold on as her ebony eyes stare with opaque unknowability. I am crying. My tears fall onto her smooth fur. She kicks. I hang on. She squirms away from my chest, and with a thrust of her head and forelegs expels herself from the womb of my embrace and leaps. I cry out, fearing a shattering of untested legs. But without a stumble she lands soundlessly on her padded feet and scampers into the willows. Beast stays by my side, no longer pulling on his torn leash as I shout, "Come back. Come back. You're going the wrong direction. The coyotes will eat you." My cries return to me in repeating, fading sound waves. Alice has stepped through the looking glass without a backward glance.

The willows surrender no clues to assist me in the search. Not so much as a rustle or quiver. I will never find her, never know whether maternal instinct or the hunger of the pack prevailed. The scent of human-canine contamination could lure her mother or her executioner to her side.

I was just a child when Tweedledum and Tweedledee foretold Alice's destiny as a figment of a mad king's dream, a pawn in a topsy-turvy game of chess. Even though the Alice of my youth will never return from the looking glass, she will reach the end of the board, as the story goes, to claim her queen's crown. Of that I feel surprisingly confident. Isn't that what we all deserve, whether or not we realize it, for embarking on the journey in the first place? We have no maps for guidance, no knowledge beforehand of the destination. And yet we forge ahead.

The willows retain their prize. I turn my back, pulling Beast with me, drying my tears in the breeze. We have a mile to go, and Jake and Nan, having packed up our campsite by now, are probably waiting for us at the car. Beast detects an intriguing scent and doesn't look back either, his prey forgotten or the chase no longer of interest.

The creek bed widens into an actual trail that surmounts one last knoll before merging with the road. And then I hear it. A muffled, persistent roar. I turn back toward the mountain and walk back up the creek bed and around the bend into another channel. A waterfall spills down a ravine, suffusing everything it touches with the possibility of life. I head up in search of the source—perhaps the sparkle of emerald green that caught my eye on the summit.

The splash of tumbling water subsides as the grade eases. In the basin above the ravine, the stream runs pure and melodious, flowing out of a lake cupped between the rock debris of a Pleistocene glacier and the precipitous eastern slope of the mountain we climbed. I stand trans-fixed before two reflections captured in its liquid mirror: the mountain and mine. The mountain so huge, my silhouette so small, I feel like I could reach into the water and caress its submerged shoulders, and some universal, transcendent truth would bubble up to the surface. The mountain's reflection stretches across from the opposite shore. Windblown waves ripple the water without disturbing either of our reflections. I take off my pack and kneel, inhaling the cool dampness. I could be an ephemeral cloud or a rock that tumbled down to the shore or a churning wave. My shadow has shrunk to a featureless face, shorn of self-obsession and the various masks I've worn, confusing them for my original face before I was born.

"You describe it in vain, you picture it to no avail," Zen master Mumon Ekai wrote centuries ago. "Praising it is useless, cease to worry about it at all. It is your true self, it has nowhere to hide. Even if the universe is annihilated, it is not destroyed."

The wind stirs and shifts, piloting the waves in the other direction. They carry me across time, to the opposite shore, washing away mortal concerns, lightening a heavy load. The weight of my fallible judgment, the mutual treachery that destroyed our marriage lifts. I think of Mumon's contemporary Dōgen and his teaching. How we must make mistake after mistake until we realize how hopelessly lost we are. In this light even the rogues of history seem worthy of forgiveness. The conquistadors for the savagery of their conversions. The gold miners for the wreckage of their greed. A mantra of compassion rises to my lips for George Ruxton, rasping and delirious in his Saint Louis hotel room in August 1848, his dream of a second trip to the Colorado Rockies ebbing away in the effluvia of terminal dysentery. And for Isabella Bird dying of heart disease in an Edinburgh nursing home in October 1904, one week shy of her seventy-third birthday, her packed trunks in London awaiting her departure for China for that long-coveted Trans-Siberian train trip to Mukden.

The real mountain draws my gaze upward into its immense face. Even if I wanted to, I cannot hide. Not here, not before any mountain I have climbed over the past forty years. In this raw landscape, where the earth is folded up into the sky, you are at the mercy of the wind and the hail and the thunder. At the first whiff of ozone as the clouds thicken and roil, the hair stands up on your forearms like porcupine quills, and you're running, running for your life. And still the lightning may hunt you down, the stunted trees of little help. The wind blows away the cloud cover as it scrubs you clean. The piercing light scatters the shadows, shining its luminosity on you.

I used to think I could leave my mark. But soon after my passage my tracks fade into the past. And all those scrawled signatures in summit registers—mere pencil on paper, as transitory as the aspen leaves that burst into being in June only to decay beneath my feet by October. The mountains have left their mark, reshaping me in their image. They've lifted me up, worn me down, carved a lifetime of triumphs and defeats, joys and sorrows into my skin. My heart, even with its old scar tissue, beats with faithful efficiency. My feet are less steady but my footing is more secure. When the rock slides out from under me, I sacrifice hard-won ground but I'm still standing.

"Jane! Jane!" Is that Jake calling my name? So poignantly reminiscent of my father. *Woof, woof, woof.* My loyal dog perhaps. Or his untamable ancestor? I listen hard. But the sounds are too indistinct, too muddled with the burbling stream to be certain. The breeze ruffles the purple columbines, runs its icy fingers through my hair. I zip up my jacket to stifle the shivering, then look over my shoulder for a flash of silver, half hoping a coyote will appear so he can stir me, with his primeval bark, out of my dream and turn me toward home.

Epilogue

June 2016: I'm looking up flight schedules at the library when my cell phone rings. It's Mother. She doesn't have to tell me why she's calling. Her weeping communicates more than words.

We knew it was coming but not this soon. In October Alice refused the mastectomy prescribed for the tumor in her breast, her second in five years. "You're not going to cut it off," she said, wide-eyed, her hand clutching her breast. In May she rejected the pacemaker and oxygen the cardiologist prescribed after she was rushed to the emergency room with shortness of breath. Alice was adamant. "No, no, no!" The surgeon respected her wishes; the cardiologist snapped at Mother, Alice's guardian, "Do you understand what this means?"

That was the question I was going to ask Alice when I got to Kansas City. I wanted to make certain. "She knew, maybe not at the level you or I would understand, but she knew. She just couldn't articulate it," my friend Nan, a hospice veteran, assures me.

After breakfast Alice wheeled her wheelchair to her spot beside the nurse's station—her asylum from the drilling and pounding and choking dust of a lobby under reconstruction. She didn't make a sound as her fellow residents shouted for their meds and clustered in the hallway by the nurse's station, jostling for their spot away from the bedlam. Alice was the quiet one who rarely asked for anything, who gave everything away. The lavender nightgowns and shirts—her favorite color—that Mother bought her and the postcards of Longs Peak I sent didn't remain in her possession for long. Even her dentures ended up in someone else's mouth.

They thought she was napping. She often napped after eating. For some time she slumped slightly to one side, her head drooping. An aide wondered and put a stethoscope to her heart.

Mother found a crumpled dollar bill on her dresser. "That's all she had. One dollar to buy some candy. No wonder she hoarded it."

It pleases me that Alice got to eat one last meal before dying.

After Labor Day I will scatter her ashes with Dad's at Hollowell Park, the dried-up grasses as golden as any crown. This time I will fulfill my promise. I didn't make that trip to Rocky Mountain National Park after his memorial service. I kept putting it off. The traffic in Denver. My lousy night vision. Where would I camp in Estes among all those motels and condominiums? And a host of other excuses.

The other day I bumped into Dad at the grocery store while inspecting bananas for bruises. An elderly gent shuffled by, chin stuck to sternum, bowed legs stiffer than a bucked bronco rider. Dad's labored gait. Yesterday I glimpsed Alice at a stoplight. A toothless woman in rags pawed at an orange. A passing driver must have tossed it out his window after spotting her sign. "Hungry!" I felt nothing but sympathy. That's all I had to offer.

They live in my stories, their perseverance in the face of adversity a powerful antidote to the temptation of the looking glass.

Timeline

Winter 1847	George Ruxton hunts along the Front Range, camping for several weeks at the foot of Pikes Peak.
August 1848	George Ruxton dies in Saint Louis of dysentery.
September 1873	Isabella Bird arrives in Colorado.
October 1873	Rocky Mountain Jim guides Isabella up Longs Peak.
1879	*A Lady's Life in the Rocky Mountains* is published.
June 1880	Isabella's sister, Henrietta, dies.
March 1881	Isabella marries Henrietta's physician, John Bishop.
March 1886	John Bishop dies.
November 1892	Isabella Bird is the first woman to be elected a fellow of the Royal Geographical Society.
October 1904	Isabella dies a week before her seventy-third birthday.
August 1954	The author's first trip to Rocky Mountain National Park at age three.
August 1960	Dave Rearick and Bob Kamps make the first ascent of the Diamond on Longs Peak.
Summer 1974	Karl introduces the author to Colorado's fifty-four fourteeners.
July 1975	The author marries Karl in Cripple Creek.
July 1976	A flood in Big Thompson Canyon during Colorado's centennial celebration kills one hundred forty-three people.
June 1979	The author and Karl climb Dallas Peak, the toughest of Colorado's one hundred highest peaks.

October 1981   The author and Karl finish Colorado's one hundred highest peaks.

July 1990   The author and Karl divorce.

July 1991   The author completes the two hundred highest peaks of Colorado.

October 1994   The author moves to Utah.

Summer 2002   The Hayman fire in Colorado's Tarryall Mountains combusts into the largest wildfire in state history to date.

July 2012   The author moves back to Colorado.

Notes

Many of the following notes to *Off Trail* are keyed to the text by page number and the phrase to which the note applies.

Epigraph

vi   *"I still vote civilization"*   Isabella L. Bird quotes, *Goodreads*, www.goodreads.com/author/quotes/2995242.Isabella_L_Bird.

Part I. The Chase

Indispensable to natural history references throughout the book were Ray J. Davis, *A Field Guide to Rocky Mountain Wildflowers* (Boston: Houghton Mifflin, 1963); Ann Zwinger, *Beyond the Aspen Grove* (New York: Harper & Row, 1981); Ann Zwinger and Beatrice Willard, *Land above the Trees: A Guide to American Alpine Tundra* (New York: Harper & Row, 1972).

1   *"Would you tell me, please"*   Lewis Carroll, *Alice's Adventures in Wonderland*, Literature Project, chapter 6, www.literatureproject.com/alice/.

2. Continental Divide

19   *"Where will you be?"*   Lewis Carroll, *Through the Looking-Glass*, chapter 4, Project Gutenberg, www.gutenberg.org/ebooks/12.

3. Queen of the Mountain

For the first ascent of the Diamond on Longs Peak, I consulted David Rearick, "First Ascent of the Diamond, East Face of Longs Peak," *American Alpine Journal* 12, no. 2 (1961); Robert Kamps and David Rearick, "Report of the First Ascent of the Diamond," *Trail and Timberline* (Colorado Mountain Club), September 1960; Rudy Chelminski, "Climbers Conquer 'Impossible' Diamond," *Rocky Mountain News*, August 4, 1960; Rudy Chelminski, "Two Climbers Inch towards Summit of Longs Peak," *Rocky Mountain News*, August 3, 1960; Rudy Chelminski, "Two Start Climb on East Face of Longs Peak," *Rocky Mountain News*, August 2, 1960; Ted Dutton, "'No Climb in Nation Hard as the Diamond,'" *Denver Post*, August 4, 1960.

6. Roped

My source for George A. F. Ruxton's 1848 trip to the Colorado Rockies was his book, *Ruxton of the Rockies* (Norman: University of Oklahoma Press, 1976).

7. Souljourners

For details about Isabella Bird's time in Estes Park, I relied on Glenda Riley and Richard Etulain, eds., *Wild Women of the Old West* (Golden, Colo.: Fulcrum, 2003); Harold Dunning, *The Life of Rocky Mountain Jim* (Boulder, Colo.: Johnson, 1967); Isabella Bird, *A Lady's Life in the Rocky Mountains* (Norman: University of Oklahoma Press, 1960); Isabella Bird, *Letters to Henrietta*, edited by Kay Chubbuck (Boston: Northeastern University Press, 2002); Janet Robertson, *The Magnificent Mountain Women: Adventures in the Colorado Rockies* (Lincoln: University of Nebraska Press, 1990); John Pickering, "Isabella Bird's Desperado: The Life and Death of Rocky Mountain Jim," in *This Blue Hollow: Estes Park, the Early Years, 1859–1915* (Niwot: University of Colorado Press, 1999).

43 *"I must confess the very happiest moments"* Quoted in Richard King,"Obituary Notice of Lieutenant George A. F. Ruxton," *Journal of the Ethnological Society of London, 1848–1856*, vol. 2 (1850): 151.

44 *mountains that "upheave themselves"* Bird, *A Lady's Life*, 30.

44 *"the splintered, pinnacled, lonely, ghastly, imposing summit"* Bird, *A Lady's Life*, 55.

44 *"I did wild things"* Bird, *Letters to Henrietta*, 103.

45 *"I have just dropped into the very place I have been seeking"* Bird, *A Lady's Life*, 73.

47 *"the Mountainous One"* George Kingsley, *Notes on Sport and Travel* (London: Macmillan, 1900), 179.

47 *"The spice, the pepper and the brains"* *Boulder County News*, June 21, 1873, cited in Robertson, *The Magnificent Mountain Women*, 8.

48 *"We rode upwards through the gloom"* Bird, *A Lady's Life*, 87.

49 *"My feet were paralyzed"*; *"A woman is a dangerous encumbrance"*; *"If it isn't to take a lady up"* Bird, *A Lady's Life*, 95.

50 *"as nearly perpendicular as anything could well be"* Bird, *A Lady's Life*, 97.

50 *"I have no head and no ankles"* Bird, *A Lady's Life*, 94.

52   *"For five minutes at the camping ground"*   Bird, quoted in Barr, *A Curious Life for a Lady: The Story of Isabella Bird* (New York: Doubleday, 1970), 73.

8. Choking

55   *"had grown grown old and haggard"*   Bird, *Letters to Henrietta*, 174.
55   *"I cannot but think"*   Bird, *Letters to Henrietta*, 176.
55   *"It's killing me"*   Bird, *Letters to Henrietta*, 174
56   *"If you won't speak"*   Bird, *Letters to Henrietta*, 174.
56   *"He is a man whom any woman might love"*   Bird, *Letters to Henrietta*, 175.
56   *"I despise a man of your intellect"*   Bird, *A Lady's Life*, 247.
56   *"It binds me hand and foot"*   Bird, *A Lady's Life*, 215.
56   *"The Rocky Mountains and all that they enclose"*   Bird, *A Lady's Life*, 249.

10. Slippery

For background I relied on "Big Thompson Flash Flood of 1976," National Atmospheric Center (NOAA), Boulder, Colo., www.noaa.gov/story5688; Dunning, *The Life of Rocky Mountain Jim*; Kingsley, *Notes on Sport and Travel*; Pickering, "Isabella Bird's Desperado."

74   *"Don't let anybody think that I was in love"*   Letter from Isabella Bird to Ella Blackie, 1879, in Bird, *Letters to Henrietta*, 199.
74   *"the general ability of women to contribute to scientific geographical knowledge"*   George Curzon, Letter to Editor, *London Times*, May 30, 1893.

12. Off Belay

Isabella's account of seeing Rocky Mountain Jim in her hotel room comes from Isabella Bird, "The Visitation of Rocky Mountain Jim," *Phantasms of the Living*, edited by Edmund Gurney, Frederick Meyers, and Frank Podmore (London: Rooms of the Society for Psychical Research, 1886).

82   *"drunk with loss"*   Letter from Isabella Bird to Ella Blackie, quoted in Barr, *A Curious Life*, 189.
82   *"I'm scarcely a marrying woman"*   Quoted in Barr, *A Curious Life*, 183.
83   *"I will be with you always"*   Paraphrased in Evelyn Kaye, *Amazing Traveler: Isabella Bird* (Boulder, Colo.: Blue Penguin, 1994), 162.
83   *"I have come as I promised"*   Bird, "The Visitation."

Part II. After the Fall

87 *"The bad news is you're falling through the air"* "Dōgen Quotes," *Goodreads*, www.goodreads.com/quotes/756164-do-not-view-mountains-from-the-scale-of-human-thought.

15. Farther off the Beaten Path

For Isabella's travels after her husband's death, I relied on Barr, *A Curious Life*, chapters 3–10; Bird, "Chronology," *Letters to Henrietta*, 310–12; Kaye, *Amazing Traveler*, sections 2–3.

16. Extremity

For wildfire scenes, I relied on "Colorado's Largest Wildfires (Burnt Area)," *Denver Post*, June 25, 2012, www.denverpost.com/ci_20934186/colorados-largest-wildfires-burn-area; Gerard Wright, "Wildfire Advances on Denver Suburbs," *Denver Post*, June 11, 2012; Joey Bunch, "Colorado Hayman Fire Set High Marks for Size, Cost, Heat and Rehabilitation," *Denver Post*, June 8, 2012; Joey Bunch, "Colorado's Massive Hayman Fire Seared in Memories of Victims," *Denver Post*, June 8, 2012; John Ingold, "Decade after Hayman Fire, Questions Linger about Fire's Start," *Denver Post*, June 3, 2012; USDA Forest Service, "Hayman Fire Case Study: A Summary," USDA Forest Service Gen. Tech. Rep. RMRS-GTR-114, 2003, www.fs.fed.us/rm/pubs/rmrs_gtr114/rmrs_gtr114_001_032.pdf.

17. Pinned Again

117 *"floods of golden glory"*; *"rose-lit summits"*; *"the land nearer now in all its grandeur"* Bird, *A Lady's Life*, 86.

18. Homecoming

The following informs this last chapter: Koun Franz, "One Continuous Mistake," *Nyohō Zen*, April 1, 2016. https://nyoho.com/tag/life-is-one-continuous-mistake/.

124 *"You describe it in vain"* Mumon Ekai, *The Gateless Gate*, trans. Eiichi Shimonmisse, 1998, www.csudh.edu/phenom_studies/mumonkan/mumonkan.html.